To

....

From

....

Date

....

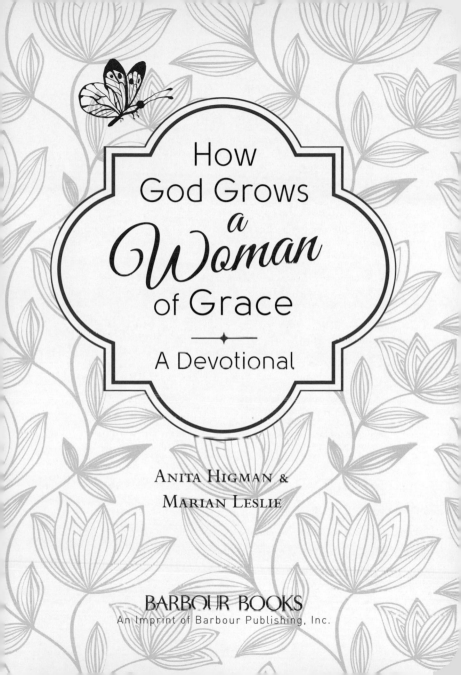

How God Grows
a
Woman
of Grace

A Devotional

Anita Higman &
Marian Leslie

BARBOUR BOOKS
An Imprint of Barbour Publishing, Inc.

Print ISBN 978-1-68322-782-3

eBook Editions:
Adobe Digital Edition (.epub) 978-1-68322-965-0
Kindle and MobiPocket Edition (.prc) 978-1-68322-967-4

Published by Barbour Books, an imprint of Barbour Publishing, Inc., 1810 Barbour Drive, Uhrichsville, Ohio 44683, www.barbourbooks.com

Our mission is to inspire the world with the life-changing message of the Bible.

Member of the
Evangelical Christian
Publishers Association

Printed in China.

To Belinda Breitling
A woman of beauty
and creativity
and abundant grace.
Know that you are greatly loved.

Anita Higman

———◆———

To Holly
For all the grace you've shown to others,
and all the grace you've been given,
and all the grace we both
yet will need (probably today).

Marian Leslie

Introduction

---◆---

The Word of God says it best. . .

*"Are you tired? Worn out? Burned out on religion?
Come to me. Get away with me and you'll recover your
life. I'll show you how to take a real rest. Walk with me
and work with me—watch how I do it. Learn the unforced
rhythms of grace. I won't lay anything heavy or
ill-fitting on you. Keep company with me and
you'll learn to live freely and lightly."*
MATTHEW 11:29–30 MSG

May we all learn Christ's
unforced rhythms of grace.

Drawing Near

"O Jerusalem, Jerusalem, the city that kills the prophets and stones God's messengers! How often I have wanted to gather your children together as a hen protects her chicks beneath her wings, but you wouldn't let me."

LUKE 13:34 NLT

It's your darling daughter's sixteenth birthday, and you feel every emotion under the sun— —affection, pride, joy, concern, delight, and a love that is so profound you know it has to be divinely designed by God Himself. Your hand goes over your heart just to think about the memories you've made and the new ones you'll have from this very day. You get a little weepy with joy as you prearrange the party chairs, and you find yourself pulling her chair just a little closer to yours. Why?

So that you will get to be a little nearer to the one you so dearly love.

Our Lord feels the same way about us—about you—which is why He's offered us such extravagant grace and such tender mercies. He wants to draw ever near because He loves us so tenderly, so protectively, so forever-ly. Won't you draw near to Him?

———◆———

Dearest Lord Jesus, in all my comings and goings and in all my daily struggles, please help me to remember how much You love me and how wonderful it is to be gathered right under the glorious wings of Your love! Amen. —A.H.

It Only Takes a Moment

*"Blessed [content, sheltered by God's promises]
are the merciful, for they will receive mercy."*
Matthew 5:7 amp

The woman behind the counter is one step away from a total meltdown. You can see it in her eyes. The way she winces in pain, you can tell her feet and her back are aching from too many long hours standing at the cash register. She had only a sliver of a smile left, and the last lady snatched it away by grumbling at her for taking too long to ring up her purchases.

You're next in line, and it looks like you have a big choice. You can either offer the woman the gift of grace and make the angels sing, or you can make her burden so great, she might break under the weight of it.

What would Christ want us to choose? Easy answer.

It takes only a moment to change a moment, a day, a life by choosing to reflect the love and mercy of Christ. Oh, how beautiful are the voices, smiles, and deeds of mercy!

*Lord, even when I'm tired and irritable, hungry and impatient,
help me to be kind in all my dealings with people—even those
who are hard to deal with. I want to be merciful to others
as You have been so merciful to me. Amen. —A.H.*

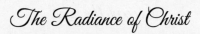

The Radiance of Christ

When Moses came down from Mount Sinai with the two
tablets of the covenant law in his hands, he was not aware that
his face was radiant because he had spoken with the LORD.

EXODUS 34:29 NIV

The light of Christ radiates onto a darkened and sin-stained world like a sunbeam bursting through a storm cloud.

As Christians, we can reflect that light of Christ. The more time we spend basking in His holy and beautiful presence, the more radiant we will become. Even if the light isn't a physical one, like Moses, there will be a brilliant joy in our countenance that will be lovely, compelling, memorable, and winsome. People will want to know what new beauty treatment we've had or if we've just gotten back from a sunny vacation at the beach.

Then we can tell them—our special light comes from spending time in the presence of the Lord. That is, singing to Him, praising Him. Getting to know His ways. Listening to His still, small voice. Being quiet before Him. Reading His living Word. Loving Him and being loved by Him. Yes, our new glow isn't just skin deep—it's soul deep!

———◆———

I love spending time with You, Lord.
My heart is full of Your joy! Amen. —A.H.

Accept the Gift!

*But the gift is not like the trespass. For if the many died
by the trespass of the one man, how much more did God's
grace and the gift that came by the grace of the
one man, Jesus Christ, overflow to the many!*

ROMANS 5:15 NIV

It arrived in the mail. Yes! It's a ticket to a glorious Christmas banquet you'd only dreamed of attending. And now, there it is, in your hands, with your name embossed across the top in gold no less. You want to RSVP immediately, but you hesitate. You don't deserve it. Why would it be completely free? Maybe it's some kind of hoax. Or maybe later you'd have to do a lot of stuff to earn it. The "or maybes" might go on for a long time, long past the banquet.

But something deep inside tells you that this is the real deal. What do you do?

RSVP. Be happy and grateful for the gift. Enjoy it. Rejoice! Know you are loved that much. And so it goes with the magnificent gift of Christ and His sacrifice. Grace so beautiful, so generous, it leaves us lit by love and light of heart.

Thank You, Lord, for Your precious and priceless gift of salvation. I do not want to live or die without it! In Jesus' name I pray, amen. —A.H.

Be the Balm

"I tell you, love your enemies. Help and give without expecting
a return. You'll never—I promise—regret it. Live out this God-created
identity the way our Father lives toward us, generously and graciously,
even when we're at our worst. Our Father is kind; you be kind."

Luke 6:36 msg

*Y*es, "that woman" has pushed you right to the very edge of your patience. Your heart is thrashing about inside your chest. Your face is flushed to a bright cherry hue. Oh, and your lips are twitching to let her have it. You have prepared a tongue-lashing she will never forget, and one that will satisfy you to the bone.

Or will it? Could it be that when bedtime comes, you'll have a restless night and a sour morning? Why? Because you'd know that even though you were provoked, your response was hurtful and not very Christlike. And you've learned from experience, that long-term regrets overshadow any false and fleeting satisfaction you get from clobbering someone with a few choice words.

So, instead of landing a verbal bomb onto someone's life, wouldn't it feel better all-around to be the balm? That is just what Christ would want from us—truth in love, yes, but also abundant grace. Which is what the Lord gives to us. . .

Jesus, when I want to lash out at those who irritate me
or wrong me, please help me respond with mercy,
forgiveness, and kindness. Amen. —A.H.

Living Large

*"And whoever wants to be greatest of all must be the slave
of all. For even I, the Messiah, am not here to be served, but to
help others, and to give my life as a ransom for many."*
MARK 10:44–45 TLB

*C*hrist came to serve, yes, but you mean *we* are to be servants too? Surely you jest! From our modern mind-set, servanthood sounds like a life of bowing and scrapping—a never-ending stream of thankless, boring chores that don't benefit us at all. No glitz. No fun. No limelight. No adventure. No creativity. No style! In other words, you can't live large when you're a servant, right?

However, God's ways are not our ways. That concept seems mysterious. Yet to surrender "our ways" to the Lord is not only possible but liberating. Watching out for other people sounds like a recipe for an unhappy life, and yet when we follow our Lord in every way, there will never be more joy, more freedom, more peace, and more real love than when we are right where God intended us to be. Our gifts will be used up. Our cup will overflow. Our lives will be rich in a thousand ways the world cannot even imagine.

Ahh yes, and how glorious it will be to hear those words from our Savior, "Well done, my good and faithful servant!" Now that is living large!

———◆———

*Holy Spirit, show me how to live a generous life of
beauty and grace and service. Amen. —A.H.*

Lavish the Love

"Let me give you a new command: Love one another. In the same way I loved you, you love one another. This is how everyone will recognize that you are my disciples—when they see the love you have for each other."

JOHN 13:35 MSG

Love.

Do your shoulders relax a little just thinking about that sentiment? They should. It's what the world needs desperately, even if people are too hurt and tired and broken to admit it.

Christ offers all of us His lavish love, and as His followers we should reflect this same benevolence. How can you show your love today?

1. Perhaps listen to a stranger's story. She might need a listening ear, a voice of compassion, and a smiling face.

2. Choose to befriend someone at your office who has no friends.

3. Reach out to your child's teacher with a random act of compassion.

4. Roll down your car window and hand that homeless woman a little care package that you've prepared in advance.

5. Visit a shut-in with a hot meal and her favorite magazine.

6. Send a note of encouragement to your pastor and your pastor's family.

7. Remind your spouse and/or best friend just how much they are loved by you!

There are hundreds of ways to show love. What does your list look like?

Holy Spirit, show me how to love all those who cross my path, that they might come to know Your light and love and grace. Amen. —A.H.

A Blank Canvas

This High Priest of ours understands our weaknesses, for he faced all of the same testings we do, yet he did not sin. So let us come boldly to the throne of our gracious God. There we will receive his mercy, and we will find grace to help us when we need it most.

HEBREWS 4:15–16 NLT

God, what shall we paint today? What are the colors of Your grace? How shall we begin?

If you were given a blank canvas, some tubes of paints, and some brushes, and you were told to paint a picture of grace, what would it look like? Would it be a pastoral scene complete with sumptuous grasses, gurgling brooks, and pudgy little lambs? Would your painting be drenched in bright, bold sweeping colors that represented the shouting vibrancy and celebratory spirit of this unmerited favor from God? Or maybe your picture would be awash with soft and mellow hues like the tranquil sigh from a thankful heart.

This beautiful thing called grace is bound to make us feel, make us search, make us rejoice. How does grace look to you on this blank canvas of your heart?

———◆———

God, I love Your mercy and Your grace. With all my soul, I thank You for Your divine gifts. In Jesus' name I pray, amen. —A.H.

Paradise Regained!

Three different times I begged the Lord to take it away. Each time he said, "My grace is all you need. My power works best in weakness." So now I am glad to boast about my weaknesses, so that the power of Christ can work through me.

2 CORINTHIANS 12:8–9 NLT

We humans long for perfection and beauty and wholeness, because that is what we were meant to know. We were not created to endure grief and suffering, and the ugliness of sin and death. We were meant to walk with God. So when we fall in body, mind, or spirit, we sense profoundly that we have suffered a horrific loss, which we have indeed! We want it all back. We want that paradise lost, as Milton called it.

Sometimes the Lord grants good health as well as other good things, and sometimes He withholds what we yearn for. Why? Because His grace is all we need. This may not be the way we want to live—that is, with some kind of misery attached to us, but no matter what happens to us, we can still call on the Lord. We can still walk in His divine presence, know Him, trust Him. We can live each day bathing in the beauty of His light and love.

He is all we need. That misery that may stay with us for a season or for life is a weakness that can highlight the power and all-sufficiency of Christ—the knowing that in our fragility, He is sublime and all we need. Christ is our everything as we wait for paradise regained!

———◆———

Lord, thank You that in my weakness Your power can work through me. Amen. —A.H.

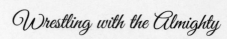

Wrestling with the Almighty

"Your name will no longer be Jacob," the man told him. "From now on you will be called Israel, because you have fought with God and with men and have won."

GENESIS 32:28 NLT

*I*f our lives were somehow connected to two big red levers and one was labeled "The World's Easy Route," and then what the Bible refers to as, "The Narrow Way," which lever would we naturally want to pull? Seems like a pretty straightforward choice.

And yet? Wouldn't it be wiser to cling to God during seasons of doubt, fear, confusion, and discouragement—and to even wrestle with Him on occasion as it mentions in Genesis 32—than to find any kind of solace in the deceptive whispers, the bogus encouragements, and the counterfeit promises of Satan?

What do you need to talk to God about today? What is keeping you from trusting Him fully with every part of your life? Be candid just as David was in the Psalms. He already knows what you're thinking, so honesty is always the only way to go.

———◆———

Lord Jesus, I admit that our culture is changing drastically and many of the disciplines and spiritual practices that are now prevalent in our society are not from You. I too find myself wanting to embrace the popular and trendy ways of the world instead of trusting You with all my life issues. Help me, Lord, to rely on You alone for all my needs. Amen. —A.H.

What We Have Forgotten

Every good thing given and every perfect gift is from above; it comes down from the Father of lights [the Creator and Sustainer of the heavens], in whom there is no variation [no rising or setting] or shadow cast by His turning [for He is perfect and never changes].

JAMES 1:17 AMP

*A*braham Lincoln said, "We have forgotten the gracious hand which has preserved us in peace and multiplied and enriched and strengthened us, and have vainly imagined in the deceitfulness of our hearts that all these blessings were produced by some superior wisdom and virtue of our own. Intoxicated with unbroken success, we have become too self-sufficient to feel the necessity of redeeming and preserving Grace, too proud to pray to the God that made us."

Great words of wisdom from our sixteenth president. Yes, if we allow the limelight of our abundant successes and blessings to go to our heads, these personal glowing victories will eventually blind us to the truth—the truth of who we really need to thank most humbly for everything we have.

———◆———

Oh Lord, I thank You for all You've given me. Your merciful grace. My precious family. My dear friends. Good work and good food. My material blessings. I praise You now and forevermore. In Jesus' name I pray, amen. —A.H.

May We Tread Lightly

Be kind and helpful to one another, tender-hearted [compassionate, understanding], forgiving one another [readily and freely], just as God in Christ also forgave you.

EPHESIANS 4:32 AMP

*R*ight before the wedding, the tired little flower girl accidentally plopped down in her basket of rose petals—the one that she was to sprinkle up the church aisle. As she stared at the crushed and bruised blossoms, sharp words were flung at her, wounding the already heartbroken girl. Hot tears then streamed down the little girl's cheeks.

Years later, a grown woman sits at her office desk, gazing off into space. She would like to think upbeat thoughts about her coworkers, her family and friends, and about herself. She would like to do well and move forward in all areas of her life, but on some days she feels snagged on the many sharp barbs from the past. In some ways, she still feels as bruised as those rose petals.

So many things can hurt us in this fallen world. May we ever tread lightly with all our deeds and words, and may they be helpful and tenderhearted and understanding.

———◆———

Holy Spirit, before I let fly with some bruising barbs, please check me and remind me how powerful and lasting words can be. May I be more like You every day. Amen. —A.H.

Hiding No More

Search me, God, and know my heart; test me and know my anxious thoughts.
See if there is any offensive way in me, and lead me in the way everlasting.

PSALM 139:23–24 NIV

Sometimes we play a hide-and-seek game with God. Only thing is—on occasion, we don't really want to be found. When we are guilty of something—maybe a lot of somethings—we don't want to face God or the consequences of our sin. Hey, we know it's going to hurt. But that kind of pain is far better to endure than the suffering of our souls when we deliberately choose to walk away from God.

For our spiritual well-being, we should all vow to take a "Hiding No More" policy when it comes to sin. When we know we've done wrong, we should go straight to the One who knows all of what we've done anyway. To the One who still loves us no matter what. To the only One who has the power to forgive us and set us back on the right path.

How about you? Will you choose to "hide no more" from God?

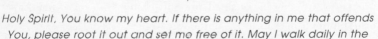

Holy Spirit, You know my heart. If there is anything in me that offends You, please root it out and set me free of it. May I walk daily in the light of Your wisdom and the beauty of Your goodness. Amen. —A.H.

When I Share

Whoever oppresses the poor shows contempt for their Maker,
but whoever is kind to the needy honors God.

PROVERBS 14:31 NIV

*H*ow many times have you wanted to give from your pocketbook to someone in need, but just as you were about to give generously you hesitated? Why? Maybe you noticed that the homeless person has just put out a cigarette, and you wondered how he had plenty of money for something that could kill him but not enough cash to buy food. Or maybe you witnessed a very able-bodied panhandler, begging for money. We've all wanted to give, but entertained thoughts similar to these. We've all wondered if he or she is actually worthy of our handout.

And yet. . .

Many of the blessings *we've* received from God—well, have they been truly deserved? If we are honest, then the answer would be no. None of us deserve anything good and lovely. All blessings in our lives come from the tender mercies of God, and He expects us to extend those same tender mercies to others.

Because to give to people who are needy honors God. To share from our storehouses, whether big or small, not only changes our fellowman, and the world, but it changes us too—all the way to the heart.

◆

Lord, teach me how to be kind and generous.
I want to be more like You, Jesus. Amen. —A.H.

Behind Closed Doors

And God is able to make all grace abound toward you, that you, always having all sufficiency in all things, may have an abundance for every good work.
2 CORINTHIANS 9:8 NKJV

Sometimes it's easy to become two people. We try to put on a sweety-peaty persona in public, but behind closed doors sometimes the "real" us emerges like a fierce dragon out of its earthen lair.

We have to ask ourselves this—who are we behind closed doors? Who are we when it's just us and God and our thought life? Who are we when it really counts? Are we women who scheme and seek to gather in glory and gratification for ourselves or are we women of true giving and grace?

That statement tends to pinch our spirits. But God sees all we do and say and think anyway. He knows the real us, and that is why He is ever working to make us more like Himself. He will not give up on us. The Lord loves us enough to keep helping us to understand the ways of heaven and the true essence of grace. *His* grace, which He gives to us freely and in abundance.

———◆———

Lord, please make me into what You created me to be and help me to be a woman of grace even when no one is looking. Amen. —A.H.

The Way We Live

*Don't cause the Holy Spirit sorrow by the way you live. Remember, he is the
one who marks you to be present on that day when salvation from sin will
be complete. Stop being mean, bad-tempered, and angry. Quarreling,
harsh words, and dislike of others should have no place in your lives.*

EPHESIANS 4:30–31 TLB

*I*t's hard to forget those "looks" from your dear old mum right after you sassed her—just because you felt like it. Or you got caught in a lie about eating that pile of cookies right before dinner. Or maybe even the time you flushed your brother's favorite action figure down the commode because he tattled on you. Yeah, you remember because that look of disappointment on your mother's face was hard to bear. You felt ashamed, since you really did know how to do right and you really did want to make her proud.

As adults have we changed all that much? We may not flush toys anymore, but sometimes we can still do things that grieve the Holy Spirit.

The Holy Spirit is the one who marks Christians to be present on that day when salvation from sin will be complete. Do we really want to cause Him any kind of sorrow?

---

*Holy Spirit, I am so sorry for all the bad-tempered things I do.
Caution me when I get too close to doing what makes You
grieve. And when I transgress, I welcome Your discipline
because I know it is for my good. Amen. —A.H.*

How Much Is Too Much?

*If anyone has material possessions and sees a brother or sister in need
but has no pity on them, how can the love of God be in that person?*
1 JOHN 3:17 NIV

*S*hop till you drop. Mmm. Does life get any better than that? Yes, shopping sprees can be oodles of fun, but how much is too much? That question will always need to be determined between you and God, but sometimes we can see hints of personal excess. Perhaps when we continually have to throw stuff out because we have an insatiable need to upgrade—everything. Maybe when we have so much food stocked in our pantries that it goes to waste. Or when we see great need all around us and we choose to shrug rather than share. Those might be clues that we should pray about how we spend our cash.

All the money we have is a blessing from God. All that we have is not ours forever, but borrowed only for a time. We are not owners but stewards. Sharing is not only the good and godly choice, it is the way of joy, of peace, of love and grace. Does life get any better than that?

---◆---

*Lord, give me a heart to share what I have with those who are needy.
Give me wisdom and discernment in my giving and also a generous
and compassionate nature. In Jesus' name I pray, amen. —A.H.*

Something Wonderful in Mind

"Do not judge by appearance [superficially and arrogantly],
but judge fairly and righteously."
JOHN 7:24 AMP

*H*umans are fascinating creatures, aren't they? We have the ability to watch a stranger walk into a room and assess her from top to toe in a matter of seconds. We can do lightning-speed appraisals concerning education, beauty, grooming, intelligence, dress, fitness, and productivity to name a few. Yes, we can judge, understand, and fully evaluate the level of her worthiness to be in our company within the blink of an eye. Or not.

The Bible says we might try to do that very thing, but we are not to judge by appearance. Why? Because to do so would be superficial and arrogant, and most of the time our opinions would be fallible.

This person—whom you dismissed—may have been placed in your path to become your new business associate, your prayer partner, your client, or your new best friend. God may have something wonderful in mind for you both, so choose to set aside those hasty and shallow judgments so you can come to know the beauty of the relationship you almost missed out on.

Oh Lord, I am guilty of making quick judgments. Please help me
to be wise and fair in all my dealings with people.
In Jesus' name I pray, amen. —A.H.

Growing in Beauty and Grace

*But grow [spiritually mature] in the grace and knowledge of our Lord
and Savior Jesus Christ. To Him be glory (honor, majesty, splendor)
both now and to the day of eternity. Amen.*

2 PETER 3:18 AMP

*G*etting to know other people isn't easy. We might even have trouble getting to know ourselves! But what if we do know what we are about—the real us deep down? Do we ever gaze into the mirror and think, *This me I see isn't all that wonderful?* What then?

If we're honest, we've all had those days when we know we're not acting like mature Christians. We're not growing with grace as we had hoped. We've let a lot of people down, including ourselves. We know it's in us to be so much more, but we don't know how or where to start. We need a holy nudge.

God is the only One who can grow us into women of spiritual beauty and grace. He is the only One who can supernaturally change us. Shall we let Him? Let's ask Him how we can begin.

---◆---

*Oh Lord my God, please help me to be all that You created me
to be—a woman of integrity and generosity and compassion.
Make me into Your kind of wonderful. Amen. —A.H.*

A Heart Full of Joy

Those of us who are strong and able in the faith need to step in and lend a hand to those who falter, and not just do what is most convenient for us. Strength is for service, not status. Each one of us needs to look after the good of the people around us, asking ourselves, "How can I help?"

ROMANS 15:1–2 MSG

*H*ave you ever known regret? Everyone has. Sometimes we regret not lending a hand to people when they're in obvious need. Or not saying, "I'm sorry," or "I love you," enough. Or we withhold something good or an encouraging word when we could have been such a blessing in someone's life. Or we fail to tell someone the good news of Christ. Why do we act in ways that are contrary to the Word of God? Is it from apathy or laziness? Disobedience? Illness or exhaustion?

As Christians, we should ask ourselves how we can infuse our daily lives with these verses from Romans. Ask the Lord for the courage to say, "How may I help you?" Then pray for the strength to carry out whatever is needed.

May we come to the end of our lives not with a heart full of regret but a heart full of joy!

Lord, give me the will, the courage, and the strength to be the help and encouragement that people need all around me. Amen. —A.H.

Keeping It Real

We are all infected and impure with sin. When we display our
righteous deeds, they are nothing but filthy rags. Like autumn leaves,
we wither and fall, and our sins sweep us away like the wind.
ISAIAH 64:6 NLT

There is a little sass in the way she sashays down the hospital hallway and in the way she shows off that impressive vase of roses that she brought for her friend in room 223. This will, after all, officially make three random acts of thoughtfulness in one month. Imagine! She may even get the Volunteer of the Year award from her church. Such an honor. She already sees herself walking up to the stage—looking surprised and humble of course—as she receives the prestigious award. In fact, in her spare time she's been working on an acceptance speech. She wonders if she should even get a new dress for the big event.

Then she suddenly trips in the hospital hallway, nearly sending her bouquet flying out of her hands. Could that be a slight caution from God concerning her attitude? It certainly would be a good time to pause and ponder one's motivations. Maybe the sweet fragrance of her good deeds was getting a bit fouled with pride, ambition, and ulterior motives. So what can be done for her—for all of us?

Be real before God. Confess. And then let Him show us how compassion is really done.

---◆---

Lord, I'm sorry for the pride that gets mixed up with my good deeds.
Help me to be more like You in all my endeavors! Amen. —A.H.

Extending Grace

Let no corrupt word proceed out of your mouth, but what is good for
necessary edification, that it may impart grace to the hearers.
EPHESIANS 4:29 NKJV

*A*fter another quick time check, you've now waited in the "returns line" seventeen minutes and thirty seconds. The line is barely moving. You've wrinkled your brows, tapped your shoe, and in about one more minute you're going to let somebody have it. After all, they're wasting *your* valuable time! What do you need to offer instead of a load of damaging verbiage?

Grace.

Or, maybe you've spent all morning making a cherry pie with the perfect filling and flakiest crust to give to your new neighbor, just to hear her say, "Too bad cherry isn't my favorite pie." What would be far better than a twitch of the eye and a prickly comeback?

Grace.

Yes, it's the same good stuff God offered us when we fell into spiritual trouble time and time again. It's the same good stuff He expects us to offers others. Grace. Is it always easy? No. Is it always beautiful? You already know the answer.

Lord God, the next time I feel like decimating someone with my harsh words, please let me calm down and remember all the many times You offered me the gift of grace when I didn't deserve it. Amen. —A.H.

Wonders

God looked over everything he had made; it was so good,
so very good! It was evening, it was morning—Day Six.
GENESIS 1:31 MSG

A new day. Got it. Alert? Maybe not. Need a mug of beefy brew. Okay. Head down. Driven. Robotic routine now in motion. And that's just breakfast time! Humans tend to forget to look up as they bulldoze through their hours, their days, their years. And we all have stress-filled lives and disease-laden doctor's reports to prove it.

Couldn't we just pause and ponder for a bit? Stroll or swing for a spell? Perhaps even look up sometimes? Take note of all the many and miraculous wonders God gave us? Could we not let our spirits dance a little from all the sublime handiwork around us? Some of them are everyday marvels, and some are not so familiar and enchantingly peculiar.

We have rainbow eucalyptus, poodle moths, light pillars, shoebill birds, pink lightning, frost flowers, mantis shrimp, flammable ice bubbles, and thorn bugs to name a few of the more intriguing and mystifying elements of nature. Go online and type in the words "phenomenon in nature" and see what other spectacular oddities God would love for you to discover!

On days that feel too driven or mundane, may we pause to ponder all that the Almighty has given us to delight in. This world is full of gasping mysteries!

———◆———

Lord, I am awestruck and so thankful for Your glorious,
ingenuous, and imaginative handiwork! Amen. —A.H.

Those Big Honking Weeds

*If we confess our sins, he is faithful and just and will forgive us
our sins and purify us from all unrighteousness.*

1 JOHN 1:9 NIV

*A*hh, spring—a time for the earth to reawaken from its slumber. Grasses push up lush and bunny soft while blousy blooms get all heady with perfume. But before we can enjoy the vibrant lawns and gardens, we have some serious tidying to do on those neglected beds. While we looked the other way, big honking weeds have been growing wild with abandon and even in places we didn't expect. They will need to be yanked out—and not superficially, but with sincere intent—by digging deeply and taking them out by their roots.

Easy to accomplish when cleaning up the garden for spring. Not so easy when contemplating our spiritual lives and the missteps, failings, and sins that have been allowed to take root while we were busy not paying attention. The good news is that God will come to our aid with all that we need to make things right again—to return our spiritual garden to the beautiful state it was meant to be in.

Shall we let Him? The Lord is excited to get started!

Holy Spirit, please show me all the ways I've grieved You with my transgressions. Remove any sins that have taken root in my life. Please forgive me. Thank You for being faithful to set me free! Amen. —A.H.

Rosebuds Left by the Front Door

*Never let loyalty and kindness leave you! Tie them around your neck
as a reminder. Write them deep within your heart.*

PROVERBS 3:3 NLT

*K*indness has become like a treasure buried away in the attic. You discover an old wooden chest, lift the lid, and there between the layers of tissue papers are hidden splendors. Wonderful memories that warm your heart and bring you joy. In our world of waywardness and selfishness and vindictiveness, this is how kindness has become—faded and almost forgotten.

With the Lord's help, kindness cannot only be revived, it can become a way of daily life. How? Be the first wherever you go. Step out and follow through with those heartfelt deeds, even when you don't feel like it. Do them for strangers and neighbors. Do them for your mom and dad, sisters and brothers. Do them for your kids. Do them for your pastor and the newcomers at church.

As Proverbs reminds us, "Never let loyalty and kindness leave you! Tie them around your neck as a reminder. Write them deep within your heart."

—◆—

*Lord, I want kindness and loyalty to be so much a part of my daily
life that these actions come naturally to me. Together we
can make kindness cool again. Amen. —A.H.*

Celebrate with Me

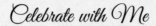

"Or imagine a woman who has ten coins and loses one. Won't she light a lamp and scour the house, looking in every nook and cranny until she finds it? And when she finds it you can be sure she'll call her friends and neighbors: 'Celebrate with me! I found my lost coin!' Count on it—that's the kind of party God's angels throw every time one lost soul turns to God."

LUKE 15:8–10 MSG

Grace comes in many forms, but the greatest is God's grace. It goes far beyond our meager mercies. It goes beyond the very best we can conjure up or imagine. It goes beyond all the loftiness and noblest and grandest of human offerings.

It is the unmerited favor of Almighty God.

There is nothing He won't do, nothing He will withhold to bring a lost soul to Himself. He was willing even to sacrifice His only Son. He loves in a way we cannot fathom and cannot replicate. But we can do one thing—accept it.

When you do turn to God and accept His redemption through Christ, know that there is a celestial celebration—a party like none other. Celebrate with Him. The angels surely do.

---◆---

Oh Lord, I'm grateful that You loved me dearly enough to come and find me. To offer me Your grace, Your redemption, and Your promise of eternal life! Amen. —A.H.

No Matter Who You Are

For everyone has sinned; we all fall short
of God's glorious standard.
ROMANS 3:23 NLT

*I*n an old telephone joke, the prankster calls someone randomly and with an ominous tone says something like, "I know what you've done. And I'm going to tell."

Think about it. No matter how faithful you are on that church pew, no matter how much money you give to charity, no matter how many degrees you have in theology, that telephone call will probably send chills running down your back. Not just because the call is creepy, which it is, but because people can't help but feel guilty about something. Well, that is because we are guilty of something. To be honest, we are all guilty of a lot of somethings!

Thank God for grace. We need it. Every day, every hour, we need the Lord. If you think you're already pretty close to perfection, think again. If you imagine yourself making it through this life without God's grace, you're lost on the journey before you've even gotten started.

Life may seem complicated, but it's also simple. Go with God. Go with grace.

◆

Oh Lord, I am humbled by Your compassion toward me,
and I am wowed by Your grace. Amen. —A.H.

The Secret Room

"And you may be sure that your sin will find you out."
NUMBERS 32:23 NIV

*I*n the new-home building market, it has become popular to add a secret room to people's houses. The entrance to this special place may have been constructed to look like an ordinary wall with shelving, but with the mere pull or push of one's fingertips, a door magically opens to reveal what has been hidden—a hidey-hole to conceal oneself away from intruders. Brilliant move, really.

When it comes to sinning, we try to construct the same secret room in our souls. Not so brilliant. Do we really think we can transgress all over the place and then hide it from God? He is omnipresent and all-knowing, so it's absurd to think we're going to get away with anything ungodly on the sly. His way of living is the only way—which is full of light and truth and beauty and love. All the good stuff. All the stuff we crave deep in our souls even though we try to hide that longing too.

So, let us fling open wide that secret room in our souls and let God move in with His grace. It will be the most beautiful cleanup of a lifetime!

———◆———

Lord, I'm sorry for the sins I've tried to keep hidden from You.
Please forgive me, and set me free from this path of folly. Amen. —A.H.

Those Beautiful Roses

*"Stand up in the presence of the aged, show respect for
the elderly and revere your God. I am the Lord."*

LEVITICUS 19:32 NIV

That bouquet of roses you bought is now looking kind of droopy and faded. They're not as lush or fragrant as they used to be. The wow factor is gone, so you go ahead and chuck them in the trash. But then later you remember that those roses can be quite wonderful dried, tied with pretty ribbons, and hung upside down to give your kitchen that cool French country look. Too late. The roses are gone.

Sometimes it feels as though society treats the elderly in the same manner as the wilted roses. We no longer think they have much wow factor left, so perhaps we don't value them as we should.

Just consider what amazing lessons of grace are held in their still-sharp minds. Tell them your stories and listen to theirs, and drink in the wisdom of years of walking in this world. And even when they can no longer speak or make connections, we can hold their hands and look into their faces, lined with years, and see their value through the eyes of God. Each human, no matter the age, is made in God's image and is precious in His sight. And they should be precious in our sight as well.

---◆---

*Thank You, Lord, for the blessing of grandparents.
May I always honor and love them as I should. Amen. —A.H.*

The Gifts of the Kingdom

God, you did everything you promised, and I'm thanking you with all my heart. You pulled me from the brink of death, my feet from the cliff-edge of doom. Now I stroll at leisure with God in the sunlit fields of life.

PSALM 56:13 MSG

The closer sin and darkness get to the light, the more they squirm with conviction. The more they want to flee deeper into the shadows.

That is because our human souls were never meant to be blackened with malevolence. We were meant to walk in the light of God's presence and receive the gifts of His kingdom. Because as we walk with Him, we learn. We grow. We see truths that were right before us but could not be comprehended. We come to see beauty all around us. We experience love like nothing else known on earth. Yes, in that light of His presence we can talk with Him, ask about the mysteries of the universe, talk about our trials and triumphs and the glorious kingdom that is to come!

As it says in Psalm 56, may we always stroll at leisure with God in the sunlit fields of life.

Oh Lord, remind me daily how important it is to stay near You and walk ever in Your light and love. Amen. —A.H.

A Toxicity of the Soul

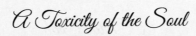

Religion that God our Father accepts as pure and faultless is this:
to look after orphans and widows in their distress and to
keep oneself from being polluted by the world.

JAMES 1:27 NIV

Today's news is loaded with dire warnings and admonishments on the subject of our toxic environment. We have air pollution, noise pollution, water and soil and even space pollution. We have carelessly dumped and poisoned and cut down God's beautiful garden called earth. In short, we have made a mess.

But even though we are to be concerned about being good stewards with what God has entrusted to us, how many news articles are written on how the world is full to the brim with spiritual pollution of every kind? In fact, there is more than enough sin and darkness and evil to make us quite sick. Should we not be more concerned about the contamination of our eternal souls?

In God's living Word, He has made it clear how we are to live, so may we always follow His guidance and concern ourselves not only with the beauty of our planet but the beauty of our souls.

Holy Spirit, guard me from the toxic sin of this world that I might remain true to You and Your holy precepts all the days of my life. Amen. —A.H.

A Total Crab

Better to live in a desert than with a quarrelsome and nagging wife.
PROVERBS 21:19 NIV

You see a crab on the sand and, being curious, you approach it, only to have the nasty little beast open its pincers as if to nip off your nose!

This verse in Proverbs might make us think of that snippy crab, and it might shame us a bit. Most women—as well as men—have been guilty of nagging at some point in their lives. We have been whiny, cantankerous, nit-picky, quarrelsome, grumbly, and all-around fusspots. Of course to continually endure any of these attitudes coming from others would then make us want to run away or hide. Or go live in the desert!

So, if we are prone to being overly critical, how can we offer grace and kindness instead of approaching a situation with our pincers ready to nip?

Tell God about it. Ask Him to forgive you and to help you get to the bottom of why you often feel quarrelsome. Then ask the Lord for His supernatural power to change. He will be more than happy to help you do it!

———◆———

*Lord, when I feel a big bout of nagging coming on, show me
how to remain grace-filled. I do want to be more like You.
Please guide me, help me, change me! Amen. —A.H.*

I Have to Have It

"Don't store up treasures here on earth where they can erode away or may be stolen. Store them in heaven where they will never lose their value and are safe from thieves. If your profits are in heaven, your heart will be there too."

MATTHEW 6:19–21 TLB

Okay, so you only have one teeny weakness—shopping. And on one of your treasure hunts, you actually encounter a purple crystal unicorn! Wow, right? You are simply dizzy with pleasure over such a find. You're not totally sure where you'll put the curio, since you have so many shelves of knickknacks that you've given up dusting long ago. Okay, so you don't really *need* a purple crystal unicorn, and it will probably end up in a garage sale, but you won't tell yourself any of that right now. Right now, you have a powerful case of the "I have to have its" and you need to feel, to buy, to own!

Then what? You'll be totally satisfied and content and happy, until you're tired of it and you glare at the crystal unicorn, wondering, "What was I thinking to buy such a hideous thing?"

Lord, I'm so sorry for all the ridiculous impulse buys that have ended up in the trash. Help me to be wise with the money You've given me. Amen. —A.H.

Taking People For Granted

Love each other with brotherly affection and take delight in honoring each other.

ROMANS 12:10 TLB

It's easy to take people for granted. We just assume that they will always be there. They will always love us. But sometimes we get too comfortable with our assumptions and let our attitudes drift into complacency. We allow ourselves to take for granted those people in our lives whom we care about. We don't call them back. We don't remind them how much we love them. We aren't generous with them or offer them tender mercies when they falter in some way. We don't pause to listen, to comfort, to grieve with them, to encourage, or to laugh with them.

Whom do you take for granted? Your spouse? Your child? Your co-workers? Your parents? Your pastor? Your best friend? God? Well, the good news is, this very day you can choose to rise up and make what was wrong into what is right.

Love them. Call them. Now.

May we all take delight in honoring each other, not just those whom we know and love, but all of humanity!

———◆———

Lord, teach me how to love my fellow man and to never take anyone for granted. And, Lord, I know I don't say it often enough, but please know that I dearly love You too! Amen. —A.H.

Prune Puree and Abundant Grace

"Be merciful, just as your Father is merciful."
LUKE 6:36 NIV

Looking now at your toddler, she looks so enchanting there, playing quietly on the floor with her dolly. But this morning's adventure, well, it was anything but enchanting. She was sitting in her high chair and apparently she had one of those experimental urges. You know, wanting to understand the various spraying, spewing, and spurting dynamics of what could happen when a jar of prune puree baby food is thrown just so.

And then there it was—sweet brown goo all over the floor, the dog, the brand-new curtains, your clothes, your hair—and even a bit dangling precariously from the ceiling like a stalactite on the roof of a cave!

Lord, have mercy.

Yes, you not only have to pray for mercy for yourself as you clean and scrub, but you have to pray that you can show mercy to your child. You'd like to scream and pull out a few graying hairs, but your true heart wants to offer mercy as God has shown you mercy when you had your own adult versions of those exploratory urges—ones that also ended badly.

Thanks, Lord, for Your never-ending mercy toward me.
May I always show that same mercy to others. Amen. —A.H.

The Awakening

Give thanks to the God of heaven. His faithful love endures forever.
PSALM 136:26 NLT

A small child hides behind the clothes in her closet. There in her cocoon, she is safe. She sheds her tears quietly, afraid to let anyone know she's crying. She cuddles her stuffed bear, wondering but not knowing why her daddy is always so angry. Why there are so many more spankings and sharp words than hugs and affection. And that same little girl grows up wondering, but not knowing, why she sees God as a Father full of punishment and judgment rather than love.

It is really no wonder at all. What we experience growing up has a profound influence on us, more than we sometimes acknowledge or even realize. That influence can distort the way we see God, and the enemy of our souls is more than willing to keep us blinded to the connection between the two.

Yes, God is a perfect balance of love and justice, because love cannot exist without justice, but our Father God *does* love us—loves you—ever so dearly.

Are you ready for the spiritual awakening that will allow you to let go of that old image of fathers and embrace the new? God's love is real, and it endures forever!

Lord Jesus, I acknowledge and accept Your love for me.
Thank You for sending me this reminder. Amen. —A.H.

We've Seen Her in Action

*But a tiny spark can set a great forest on fire. And among all the parts of the body,
the tongue is a flame of fire. It is a whole world of wickedness, corrupting your
entire body. It can set your whole life on fire, for it is set on fire by hell itself.*

JAMES 3:5–6 NLT

We've seen her in action. She is the woman —or man—who has a mouth the size of a barrel lid, and she will not shut up! She grandstands. She blows and goes. She gossips. She pontificates. She is so full of hot air that you know at any moment she will lift right off her chair and float away into the stratosphere.

You wish.

Mmm. So easy to point our fingers at the big mouths. And yet, God says that even a tiny spark from our tongues can set off deadly fires. It can corrupt our entire body, and do damage beyond our wildest imaginings. And that fire—oh that frightful and fierce fire—is from hell itself. So wisdom used even in our smallest words is wisdom indeed!

———◆———

*God, I want to be a woman of grace, so please watch over my tongue
and all that comes out of my mouth. I want to please You in all
that I do and say. In Jesus' name I pray, amen. —A.H.*

I Go to Prepare a Place

*"There are many homes up there where my Father lives, and I am going
to prepare them for your coming. When everything is ready,
then I will come and get you, so that you can always be
with me where I am. If this weren't so,
I would tell you plainly."*

JOHN 14:3 TLB

The dear woman is nearly hyperventilating with joy as she prepares for the family's arrival on Christmas morning. She has freshened the bedrooms with new linens and fluffy pillows and little treats. She has scented the house with fresh pine boughs, spiced wassail, and homemade everything. She has turkey and ham and all the fixings—all the family's favorites. A feast fit for a king. All is in readiness, and her heart is nearly bursting with love to see their faces! Who then would call her up and say they had no interest and tell her to throw it all away. The goodies. The joy. The love.

Jesus, while He was here on earth, promised that He was preparing a place for us and He would be coming back so that we could all be together. But you can refuse His offer. You can say no. You can throw away the greatest blessing of all time—eternity with God.

Christ is bursting with love to see your face. Are you excited to see His?

———◆———

*Lord, make me ready and excited for the day
when we meet face-to-face! Amen. —A.H.*

Together as Friends

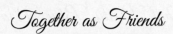

"Look! I stand at the door and knock. If you hear my voice and open the door,
I will come in, and we will share a meal together as friends."

REVELATION 3:20 NLT

*B*on voyage! It's finally the moment you and your new friend get to set sail on a cruise together. A big fancy ship with all the bells and whistles. You're so grateful to have a friend that you've paid her way—all experiences covered—even her own suite and shopping monies.

But once onboard, you don't see her much. She is so busy having a good time or tending to her own needs that you only see her in passing. You sort of get the impression she's just there for the goodies. The beauty of the sea from her private balcony, the scrumptious food, and the fun adventures. Yes, you can see, she's not interested in spending her precious time with you.

And your heart breaks.

Is that the way it goes when Christ offers us friendship with Him? We accept His grace, but then we neglect to spend time with Him? Guess we have to ask ourselves—what is more important to us—the rewards or the relationship?

———◆———

Lord, I love You. Help me to never neglect You, but instead choose
to be in constant communion with You. Amen. —A.H.

That Pretty Blue Marble

For every house has a builder, but the one who built everything is God.
HEBREWS 3:4 NLT

From space our planet looks like a pretty blue marble, sort of floating out there in the ether. The closer you come, the more you can see the beautiful details of our earth. The mighty and churning expanse of the oceans and seas teaming with every kind of creature imaginable. The mountain splendor of snowcapped summits pristine with wonder and cloaked in deep fragrant forests. More life than humans can even fully appreciate or fathom.

But also when you view life on our globe with scrutiny, you can see much more. You discover the dirty streets and dark alleys where people do what is not always pristine with wonder. You find pain and rage and lives broken with sin. Whether city or country, mankind has fallen into depravity, and we are utterly without hope except for one solitary word—*Jesus*.

As a nation, we are in desperate need to turn back to our Creator. To embrace His divine offer of grace through Christ. To follow the Lord's precepts. Only then can that pretty blue marble and all its inhabitants be all that they were meant to be.

---◆---

Lord, our nation has fallen away from You. Please give us the wisdom and courage to come home to Your love. Amen. —A.H.

A Life of Love

This is how we've come to understand and experience love: Christ sacrificed his life for us. This is why we ought to live sacrificially for our fellow believers, and not just be out for ourselves. If you see some brother or sister in need and have the means to do something about it but turn a cold shoulder and do nothing, what happens to God's love? It disappears. And you made it disappear.

1 JOHN 3:16–17 MSG

When we get up in the morning and maneuver through the day, it's easy to be consumed with well, ourselves. *Will I be recognized in my career for all my extra hours of work?. . .Will I get a raise?. . .Why can't I get my fashion act together?. . .Why are my nails always chipped and my blouse splattered with tiny coffee stains? And no matter how much I fiddle and fluff and gel my hair, why does it always look frightening?*

Our thoughts can get a bit petty at times.

So, do we live only for ourselves or do we look up and see others? Do we notice their needs and more importantly, do we do anything about it? Because of the love of Christ and His sacrifice for us, are we now living for Him? Are we living a life of love?

———◆———

Lord, show me how to not only notice the needs of others, but to have the generosity of spirit to do something about it! Amen. —A.H.

A Life of Grace

If you are wise and understand God's ways, prove it by living an honorable
life, doing good works with the humility that comes from wisdom. But if
you are bitterly jealous and there is selfish ambition in your heart,
don't cover up the truth with boasting and lying. For jealousy
and selfishness are not God's kind of wisdom. Such things
are earthly, unspiritual, and demonic.

JAMES 3:13–15 NLT

*Y*ou're strolling through your favorite forest. The breeze is cool, and the sun is warm. The air is scented with blossoms, and you feel contented all the way to your bones. Then suddenly, lying across the footpath in front of you, you spot something truly foul—a dead possum with flies buzzing all around. The smell is enough to make you wretch with disgust. Instead, you turn and run. Away. Fast.

We have all had those days when we are cruising along doing well, and then someone who is described in the above passage bursts into our space. And it's not a pretty sight. The woman or man is brimming with the nasty odor of greedy ambition, boasting, put-downs, and lies. Everything in you wants to turn and run. Away. Fast.

So, how are *we* doing? Are *we* working on a life well lived? A life of grace and beauty?

———◆———

Dear God, I need You to teach me how to live a beautiful life of
wisdom. I am willing but my flesh is weak. Please help me. Amen. —A.H.

In a Nutshell

And this is what God says we must do: Believe on the name
of his Son Jesus Christ, and love one another.

1 JOHN 3:23 TLB

*H*ow to live a better Christian life—hmm, good topic—but there are more books on that subject than people will ever be able to read in a lifetime. The volumes and videos tell us how to live more fully, more boldly, and more freely. Sometimes all the vast amount of information can be overwhelming and feel impossible to fulfill. Actually, what God asks of us *is* impossible to achieve without the supernatural power of the Holy Spirit.

But it might help for us to see that Christianity can indeed be rather simple. In a nutshell, God wants us to believe on the name of His Son, Jesus Christ, and He wants us to love one another. Because if we do this with all our hearts, all the rest will fall into place. So many of the world's problems happen because we lack faith and we lack love.

This very day, can you believe in Christ more fully and love more lavishly?

———————◆———————

God, I admit that I fail even in the most basic elements of Christianity.
Please build my faith and give me a heart full of love.
In Jesus' name I pray, amen. —A.H.

A Wonderful Moment

Give thanks to the LORD, for he is good!
His faithful love endures forever.
PSALM 107:1 NLT

Y ou spent umpteen hours working on this special present for your friend. You even sacrificed some valuable TV time to add some extra panache. But you know what? She was worth it. Every minute of every hour of it. But when the time came to present her with this one-of-a-kind love gift, well, something was missing. She smiled, held it close, and walked away with it, but she failed to say, "Thank you." What should have been a wonderful moment pierced your heart instead.

When God answers your prayer with a miracle or gives you a special gift, do you always remember to personally thank Him? The world claims all we need in this life is a grateful spirit, but that would make as much sense as thanking the air for its warmth or coolness. The acknowledgement and appreciation goes nowhere. It means nothing.

Instead, make that moment wonderful for God. Say the words that are right and good, because He is good and faithful and loving toward us, and He is worthy of our praise.

---◆---

Lord, thank You for Your mercy and grace, Your beautiful creation,
and Your many miracles and gifts to me! Amen. —A.H.

To Comfort and to Cheer

When others are happy, be happy with them.
If they are sad, share their sorrow.
ROMANS 12:15 TLB

*M*ost of the time people feel more comfortable weeping alone. They assume that no one really wants to see them cry. So they hide.

But oh, how much easier life can be when someone comes alongside us with a hand on our shoulder. Or maybe they offer us a comforting word, a listening ear, or a compassionate gesture. As Christians we should always be sensitive to those who are suffering. Those who are in chronic pain. Those who grieve. And sometimes there is more power and more compassion in sincerely weeping with someone than in thousands of words of counsel.

But sometimes when people have good news, it's even harder emotionally to cheer them on, especially if the news is glorious while we are facing hard times. And yet, with the Lord's help, we can indeed meet the needs of others, whether to rejoice or to cry.

May we rely on the strength of Christ to always find a way to weep with those who weep and rejoice with those who rejoice.

———◆———

Lord, help me to be Your instrument in this needy and broken world.
May I bring comfort and cheer whenever Your people
have need. Amen. —A.H.

The Iron Mask

When he saw the crowds, he had compassion on them because they
were confused and helpless, like sheep without a shepherd.
MATTHEW 9:36 NLT

ou've seen them. They are the folks with the iron masks. They will not allow anyone to see them in any kind of weakened condition. But if you step closer and stare for a while, you can see the cracks in their armor. You can see those flickers of fear and doubts and vulnerability deep in their eyes. It's all right there.

And sometimes that person is you.

Christ knows our frailty. He knows our confusion. He knows very well how helpless we are. But we don't need to wear a facade, pretend all is well, and merely swallow the pain. We can allow ourselves to be vulnerable and real before God. Christ has seen it all, knows it all, and incredibly, He still loves us dearly. And in the midst of that *knowing*, Christ is moved with great compassion for us. He will not leave us to wander aimlessly like sheep. He will rescue us, restore us, and refresh us. All we need to do is ask.

———◆———

Thank You, Lord, that I can come to You with my frailty,
my night terrors, and all my doubts. Thank You for loving
me enough to make me more like You. Amen. —A.H.

A Heart of Love

After that, he poured water into a basin and began to wash his disciples' feet,
drying them with the towel that was wrapped around him.
JOHN 13:5 NIV

It's hard to imagine that the Maker of the universe cared so much for His creation that He found a way to not only rescue us from our broken state, but to be closer to us, to encounter this earthly life with us.

He sent His Son to be born of a woman. To be a part of the pandemonium and wonder of growing up inside a family. To sense hunger and be satisfied by a bowl of soup. To play and feel the gentlest flutter of a butterfly's wings on His fingertip. To build furniture with His father. To laugh and love and pray through all the changing seasons. To be baptized and wash the feet of His followers. To grieve and feel those salty tears run down His cheeks over the loss of a dear friend. To understand what it's like to be abandoned, and to feel the sting of death.

Then amazingly, to do what no human could ever do—return to life and offer the world the miracle of redemption as well as friendship for all time.

That is how our Savior works. He is a most intimate God who arrived with a heart of love and a life of service.

Jesus, teach me that a life of service for Your glory
Is a life most beautiful. Amen. —A.H.

A Lighter Touch

A gentle answer turns away wrath, but a harsh word stirs up anger.
PROVERBS 15:1 NIV

*H*ave you noticed? Sometimes the new method on social media is to bulldoze through with our own agendas and our own views, no matter how brutal the comments, no matter the aftermath of destruction. After all, we have our right of free speech to protect!

Yes, free speech and truthfulness are important in all societies, but Christ has asked us to take care that we don't stoke the fires of wrath with our tantrums, which might be fueled by pride and self-centered motivations. When we allow our tempers to flare, it can burn a person's spirit for years, and it has the potential to damage a sensitive soul for a lifetime.

Hate comes so easily—too easily. May we always purify our "need to be heard" through Christ's filter of love as we ask ourselves, "Does this comment heal or hurt? Am I in a listening and learning mode, or do I just want to level someone because I'm angry at life? Am I motivated with righteous indignation to help the world be a godlier place, or do I have a stubborn need to be right?"

Yes, a gentle answer turns away wrath. It softens the situation so that all parties can reason together. May we always choose the way of grace, the way of love.

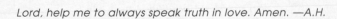

Lord, help me to always speak truth in love. Amen. —A.H.

Green and Grumpy

For everyone born of God is victorious and overcomes the world; and this is
the victory that has conquered and overcome the world—our
[continuing, persistent] faith [in Jesus the Son of God].

1 John 5:4 AMP

*D*o you ever wake up feeling green and grumpy like the Grinch? You feel tired with life, tired of people, even tired of yourself? Maybe you feel like a wimp of a Christian, failing at being a great mom, failing at being a good daughter, spouse, coworker, church member, neighbor, and citizen. You can't even make a really good bowl of soup or get your hair to go in the right direction, let alone be the matriarchal moral compass of your family and the world!

You need time-out with God.

Time for you to just be with the Lord, to bask in His light, to read His living Word, and get to know Him better. Time to be encouraged in your faith and to remember who you are in Christ. Born of God. Forgiven. Beloved. Transformed into a glorious creature who can do all things through Christ. No longer a woman just making do, but a woman of victory!

Lord, help me to remember who I am in You, a woman who
can rise up with joy and overcome! Amen. —A.H.

Renewed!

Therefore we do not become discouraged [spiritless, disappointed, or afraid].
Though our outer self is [progressively] wasting away, yet our inner
self is being [progressively] renewed day by day.
2 CORINTHIANS 4:16 AMP

*I*t hasn't been a good day. You found a new patch of gray hair. You woke up feeling creakier in your joints. And of all things, you gazed a little too deeply into that magnifying mirror only to discover that when you tug on your bottom lip, it does not spring back like it used to. It sort of hangs there kind of loose. In fact, every part of you seems to be hanging more loosely these days, and the worst part is that there isn't a lot you can do about it.

Yes, you feel your body is wasting away, as the Bible reminds you that it will, and the prospect of this "falling into ruin" phase of your life makes you feel sad, disappointed, and even terrified!

The good news—no, the *great* news—is that no matter what happens to our bodies as they age in this life, we as Christians can be constantly transformed and beautified on the inside. This is a promise. This is our hope. Praise God!

Lord Jesus, I am sad to grow old, but I choose to put my hope in You.
I will cling to Your promise that each day as I fade in mind and body,
You are renewing my inner self. Thank You! Amen. —A.H.

Because It All Matters

For by one [Holy] Spirit we were all baptized into one body,
[spiritually transformed—united together] whether Jews or Greeks (Gentiles),
slaves or free, and we were all made to drink of one [Holy] Spirit
[since the same Holy Spirit fills each life].
1 CORINTHIANS 12:13 AMP

*A*s Christians we are being spiritually transformed and united together. This concept seems mystical to us—in that we can sense it more in our spirits than we can understand it in human terms.

In a way, all humans are interrelated, because what happens to you can affect someone else, and vice versa. When you say something awful to a friend or coworker, those words don't just harm the other person; they can harm you as well. We cannot easily detach ourselves from the interactions and influences of other people. All encounters and experiences—whether good or bad—can seep deeply into our spirits, changing us for a lifetime.

So then, how should we live? Might it be best to think before we speak and pray before we charge forward? The Bible teaches us to concentrate on good and lovely things and care tenderly for others as we care for ourselves. Wouldn't that be a truly fine way to live?

---◆---

Lord, thank You for reminding me that what we think,
what we do, and what we say really does matter. Amen. —A.H.

The Problem of Pettiness

Be kind and helpful to one another, tender-hearted
[compassionate, understanding], forgiving one another
[readily and freely], just as God in Christ also forgave you.
EPHESIANS 4:32 AMP

*I*t's fun to dress up, fix up, and look into the mirror with joy. Wouldn't we ladies all like to look a bit more like a fairy-tale princess full of beauty and grace?

But no matter how much the outside gets polished, sometimes the inside still wants to spew what is far from beautiful. We might slyly give someone a backhanded compliment. Or indulge in a bout of whining or succumb to devious little mind droppings. Perhaps we'll offer a bit of gossip, juicy enough to make a saint salivate. Or perhaps we'll gloat over someone's misfortune, or become unwilling to forgive even the tiniest of offenses.

In other words, we've become a hot, petty mess.

How can you deal with the problem of pettiness? Ask the Lord to let you understand how He sees all those who cross your path. That you might see their amazing potential and how truly precious they are. Also ask Him to replace your narrow-mindedness with genuine kindness, sensitivity, compassion, and understanding. These are the kinds of prayers that will not only please our Lord but make you truly beautiful.

Lord, I am so sorry that I have been caught being petty.
Please forgive me and help me to mature as a Christian.
I desire to be more like You. Amen. —A.H.

Mutually Encouraged

I long to see you so that I may impart to you some spiritual gift to make you strong—that is, that you and I may be mutually encouraged by each other's faith.
ROMANS 1:11–12 NIV

*P*erhaps it is a grandmother or a long-time friend. Perhaps it is a former teacher or a pastor you have known. Perhaps it is a sister or brother or someone else. There are people in our lives who paint a beautiful picture of faith and grace with their lives. When we are with them, we feel the Holy Spirit filling the room. And when we are away from them, we miss that presence.

However, by telling our stories, by sharing the things that happen to us—both the good and fortunate events and the sad or disappointing ones—we can still be that encouragement for one another. We can still reveal how God is moving in our lives. And we can still demonstrate how our days are laced with grace.

Reach out to someone today. Have a chat. Post about what God has done for you. Tell your story and encourage one another.

---◆---

Lord, I'm so thankful for the people You've placed in my life to be examples to me of Your grace. I look at their lives and I am encouraged and inspired to remain faithful. Bless them, Lord. Amen. —M.L.

Sustainer

*The Son is the radiance of God's glory and the exact representation
of his being, sustaining all things by his powerful word.*
HEBREWS 1:3 NIV

*H*e was there in the beginning to speak light. And He was here on earth to bring light. Every bit of His being has shone into every crack of our world—demolishing darkness, defeating death, and redeeming our dirt.

His Word brought understanding to those who were struggling to wrap their minds around an inscrutable God. His Word brought hope to those who were at the end of their ropes. His Word brought relief to those who were struggling with illness and poverty.

His Word was food to those who were hungry for meaning. His Word was refreshment to those whose faith had dried up. His Word was life to those who were dying in sin.

What has His Word done for you?

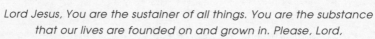

*Lord Jesus, You are the sustainer of all things. You are the substance
that our lives are founded on and grown in. Please, Lord,
keep speaking to me. I need You. Amen. —M.L.*

Gracious Conversation

Live wisely among those who are not believers, and make the most of every opportunity. Let your conversation be gracious and attractive so that you will have the right response for everyone.
COLOSSIANS 4:5–6 NLT

*H*ave you ever been talking with someone who somehow made you feel like you wanted to keep talking for a long time? Their words put you at ease, making it feel safe to even speak about important, meaningful things. Even though you may not have agreed about everything, there was a genuine spirit of willingness to attempt to understand one another. Good questions were asked. Answers were listened to. A friendship was born.

This is what gracious conversation feels like. It's conversation that leaves room for differences and yet sprouts commonalities. It's conversation that reaches across aisles, opens doors, and looks with a different perspective. It's conversation that asks for stories and wants to hear them with the same intentionality and caring as a good doctor with a patient. It's the kind of conversation that could change hearts—or lives.

Lord, examine my words. Help me to be aware of times when I say things that could be offensive or off-putting. Help me to work harder at speaking and listening in such a way as to bring people closer to You. Amen. —M.L.

Enslaved

This letter is from Paul and Timothy, slaves of Christ Jesus.
PHILIPPIANS 1:1 NLT

*I*magine you are going about your business, doing what you normally do in the regular course of your days. You get up, get dressed, have breakfast, get in your car, and go to work. But on your way, you are captured. You are taken away and put in chains. You are locked together with others. You are compelled to do other work—hard work. It's work that could be dangerous. And it's work that you don't even feel equipped to do. This is not what you signed up for. And yet, here you are. So trapped, so chained, so caught up in this new life that you couldn't escape it, even if you tried.

Imagine being so captivated by Christ that you couldn't even picture being away from Him. Imagine being so caught up in His love that you couldn't break free of it, even for a moment. Imagine being so compelled to do His will that it was as if shackles were on your hands and feet, guiding you to finish His work.

Imagine being the slave of Christ.

How far is your life from that image? How much closer would you like it to be? How do you get there?

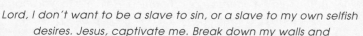

Lord, I don't want to be a slave to sin, or a slave to my own selfish desires. Jesus, captivate me. Break down my walls and take me over. Capture me! Amen. —M.L.

A New Country

*Each of us is raised into a light-filled world by our Father so that we
can see where we're going in our new grace-sovereign country.*
ROMANS 6:5 MSG

*H*ave you ever seen baby sea turtles emerging from their nest? The
wee creatures break open their shells with a sharp tooth. Then
as a group they dig their way out of the carefully concealed, underground
nest. Once they have made it out, together they head in the direction of the
brightest light. They make a mad dash for this new world, trying to avoid
death by dehydration or getting caught by predators. Life is so dangerous for
a baby sea turtle that only 1 in 1,000 makes it to adulthood.

Life is dangerous for us too. Our paths to new life in Christ are filled with
obstacles—distractions, delays, discouragements. But if we keep persevering,
if we keep shuffling our little wobbly selves toward the brightest light, we will
find ourselves in a new country—a country where grace rules. And unlike
those baby turtles, we are not left on our own to fend off predators all by
ourselves. We have a Father who is reaching out to us with open arms, longing
to gather us in, to take care of us, to heal our wounds from our journey, to
guide us, and to celebrate us!

---

*Lord, let me always see Your light and make my way
to it as fast as I can. Amen. —M.L.*

Ancient of Days

"Thrones were set in place, and the Ancient of Days took his seat."
DANIEL 7:9 NIV

*I*n Daniel 7, we read about a vision that came to Daniel as he was lying on his bed. In that vision were many curious and amazing things, but one of the most striking images is that of God, known as the Ancient of Days: "His clothing was as white as snow; the hair of his head was white like wool. His throne was flaming with fire, and its wheels were all ablaze. A river of fire was flowing, coming out from before him" (vv. 9–10).

Can you imagine? Seeing God on a throne of fire, with a river of fire following Him? Then the description goes on: "Thousands upon thousands attended him; ten thousand times ten thousand stood before him."

And we can be among those thousands. Grace is our invitation to come to the fiery party of our ancient, glorious, majestic Lord. Grace is our seat in front of Him—with a front-row view of the river of fire. And grace is our assurance that we will not be burned up, but instead be warmed and lit up with His glory!

My great and glorious God, how I long to see You! Thank You for giving me a way to meet You on Your throne of fire. Amen. —M.L.

Newborn Grace

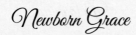

And the Word became flesh and dwelt among us, and we beheld His glory,
the glory as of the only begotten of the Father, full of grace and truth.
JOHN 1:14 NKJV

The curve of their ever-curled fingers. The pink of their flushed cheeks. The shallow, soft hollow on the top of their heads. The wrinkles in their elbows. The wet lashes stuck to their skin. The tiny, wriggling toes.

Is there anything more graceful than a newborn baby's beautiful little body? Designed so perfectly to do what it needs to do. And constructed exactly in such a way as to make us all fall in love at first sight.

What must it have been like to behold the new flesh of the Son of God? What must it have felt like to have the Almighty grasp tightly to a finger? What must it have been like to stare into the newly opened eyes of the Creator of the universe and see His truth staring back at you? Imagine for a moment holding the precious newborn Jesus in your arms.

In this little human form, God granted us all the grace any of us would ever need. Isn't that amazing?

Lord, sometimes I wish I could have known You as a baby. I wish I had had that time with You here on earth. I look forward to the day when we can walk side by side in heaven. Amen. —M.L.

Morning

For his anger lasts only a moment, but his favor lasts a lifetime;
weeping may stay for the night, but rejoicing comes in the morning.

PSALM 30:5 NIV

The first lights peep up over the clouds. Rays hit the crystal branches of trees covered in the ice storm the night before. Drip, drip, drip. The ice melts and the cold is ushered out of the air as the sun's warmth grows in strength. Snowdrifts shrink. Clear, cool water runs away, down the hill, down to the river, and away to bring its chill to other lands.

The night had brought cold and darkness. But the morning brings golden heat and light.

Again and again, morning after morning, His grace shines upon our hearts—banishing the cold anxiety and apprehensions, the darkness of our sin and doubt, and replacing it with the light of His clear truth and the warmth of His renewing love.

You can believe it. As surely as the sun will shine again tomorrow, His grace will remain.

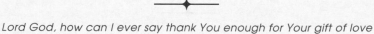

Lord God, how can I ever say thank You enough for Your gift of love
and grace and truth in my life? Whenever things seem at their darkest,
I know I can depend on You to break through and show
me the light. I will trust You, Lord! Amen. —M.L.

She Obeys

Now Esther had not revealed her family and her people, just as Mordecai
had charged her, for Esther obeyed the command of Mordecai
as when she was brought up by him.

ESTHER 2:20 NKJV

She was the queen. The Queen! She was chosen by the king from all the other lovely and favorable women who had come to his court. She was chosen. She had the king's ear. She could have done just about anything she wanted to do. She had "obtained favor in the sight of all who saw her" (v. 15).

She was a woman graced with beauty and charm. But more than that, she was a woman of grace. And a woman of grace obeys the truth.

Esther obeyed Mordecai as she had done since she was a young girl—not just because he was her authority figure or because he acted as her father. She obeyed him because she trusted him to know the truth. He was a faithful man of God. She knew she could trust him with anything—even her life.

And trusting him is what saved her life, and the lives of all her people. A woman of grace knows the truth and obeys the command of truth.

Lord, help me to study Your Word well, so I can be as familiar with
the truth as I am with my own family. Help me to
obey Your commands. Amen. —M.L.

Cleaning Day

Create in me a clean heart, O God,
and renew a steadfast spirit within me.
PSALM 51:10 NKJV

*Y*ou wipe the dust off the mantel and millions of little dust particles go flying into the air. They fall down, down, down, onto the wood floor. You sweep them up with the vacuum cleaner, but one of the vacuum's wheels leaves a scuff behind it. You bend over to rub away the scuff mark and the knees of your trousers get dirty. You throw the trousers in the washer and then the dryer, and particles go flying into the air once again.

The cycle never seems to end. Cleaning never ends. In order to really keep a house clean, you have to keep at it, day after day after tedious day.

Thank goodness God never tires of cleaning our hearts! Day after day after tedious day we ask Him to create in us a fresh, clean heart—one that desires only Him. And day after day we fail in our own efforts to stay pure.

But we can keep trying. That is why the psalmist asks for a steadfast spirit as well—it's a spirit that will steadily keep trying. A spirit that will stay strong in its will to follow God and hold fast to His commands.

God, I can't imagine why You put up with me. I fail every day to keep this heart clean. But Lord, thank You for renewing my spirit every day. I couldn't even get my laundry done without You! Amen. —M.L.

Gift of Creation

Then God said, "Let there be light," and there was light.
GENESIS 1:3 NLT

ou have all the power in Your hands. You can do absolutely anything. Anything.

And what You decide to do is create a world. You decide to create the most beautiful world ever made. And why? Because You want to create a home for people.

God didn't have to say those words. He didn't have to make this world for us. He didn't have to make us! But He did. He took all of His amazing, creative power, and formed a world that was just right for us to live and breathe in. And not only that, He made it beautiful. And not only that, He created us in His image. He made us beautiful.

And He did all this not because we had done anything to deserve it, or ever would. He did it because He wanted to love us. And He wanted us to love Him.

Creation is the first gift of God's grace. And every day, we can look around and be reminded—we can see His grace in every rock, every leaf, and every breath we take.

———◆———

Creator God, You are so amazing! Thank You for this beautiful world we live in. Thank You for the gift of light and life. Amen. —M.L.

He Broke the Bars

"I am the LORD your God, who brought you out of Egypt so that you would no longer be slaves to the Egyptians; I broke the bars of your yoke and enabled you to walk with heads held high."

LEVITICUS 26:13 NIV

The Hebrews had no reason to think they would ever get out of their situation. Even though their numbers were many, they were kept oppressed and enslaved by the Egyptians in power. They were beaten and controlled. They were regulated and impoverished. They lived in fear—of pain, of harder work, of losing their families, of having their children killed.

They had every reason to believe that they were worthless. Only cogs in a wheel they could not see. Only tools to be used by a fearsome builder.

But God showed them otherwise. He not only freed them, He enabled them to walk with heads held high. To claim a place walking beside the Lord of lords and King of kings. To be the people chosen by God.

He broke the bars that held them down and lifted them up into a new identity. And that's what He does for us too. Every day.

Lord, break whatever bars are holding me back from experiencing abundant life in You. Destroy whatever images I have in my head that keep me from living as Your child. Amen. —M.L.

Clay in the Potter's Hand

"Like clay in the hand of the potter, so are you in my hand, Israel."
JEREMIAH 18:6 NIV

Splat! The wet clay lump is thrown onto the wheel. The wheel begins to spin. The lump revolves around and around as the potter places fingers deftly onto the clay. Lines form in the brown mass. Slowly, the lump takes a shape. Graceful curves reveal themselves. What could it be? A mug? A bowl? A vase?

Then, in a flash, a finger catches on the wrong spot and what would have been a handle becomes a mangle.

The creation is ruined!

But the potter is not bothered. The wheel begins again. The lump is thrown again. Water droplets roll down and fly away as the lump spins. The skillful hands take the marred pot and reform and reshape and resculpt until once again a thing of beauty and function appears.

We are the clay. He is the Potter. And in His perfect hands any bit of our marred lives can be reshaped, reformed, and redeemed.

Lord, I want to be a functional piece in the plan of Your universe. I want to bring beauty and goodness to my world. Take me in Your hands and mold me into the form that You want me to take. Help me to see Your plan, even when all I see are my own mistakes. Amen. —M.L.

Ashamed of Grace?

For I am not ashamed of the gospel, because it is the power of God that brings salvation to everyone who believes: first to the Jew, then to the Gentile.

ROMANS 1:16 NIV

That moment comes. You are in conversation with someone and somehow the topic turns to religion. You understand that this person does not have a relationship with Christ, and you cringe at the statements they are making about believers. But what to say? What to do? You want to say something, but you don't want to be embarrassed.

Are we ashamed to speak of the grace of God? Forget about talking about what church we go to or what our personal testimony is. What about just talking about God's grace? What about talking about the gift of salvation?

"For in the gospel the righteousness of God is revealed—a righteousness that is by faith from first to last, just as it is written: 'The righteous will live by faith' " (v. 17).

We have the chance to reveal the righteousness of God, to describe His wonderful gift, and to unleash the power of God on everyone we meet who does not yet know of Jesus. What an opportunity! What's holding you back?

God, sometimes I just get stuck and can't think of the words to say to describe Your grace. Help me, Lord. Lead me to Your Word so I can reveal Your power and righteousness. Amen. —M.L.

Fake Grace

I can't believe your fickleness—how easily you have turned traitor to him
who called you by the grace of Christ by embracing a variant message! It is not
a minor variation, you know; it is completely other, an alien
message, a no-message, a lie about God.

GALATIANS 1:6–7 MSG

The power of positivity. You do you. My truth is different from your truth. There are no absolutes. You get what you put out into the universe. You are enough.

There are a lot of messages out there in the world that claim to be wisdom, or truth, or good guidance. They promise that if you follow these messages or buy these products or read these books, you will get what you want. You will be who you want to be. You will get freedom.

But the truth is, there is no way to the truth except through the Truth. There is no way to find the good life except through the Maker of all that is good. There is no way to freedom except through the One who is truly able to set us free from our sin, free from death, free from ourselves.

Grace comes from God. No one else has it. No one else is selling it. And no one else can give it. Don't believe the no-messages. Read God's Word and find the truth.

One true God, I love You. Forgive me for times when I get tempted to
follow other leaders. Forgive me when I allow my mind to get
muddled by messages that don't come from You.
Help me to seek the truth always. Amen. —M.L.

Leaky Grace

" 'Shouldn't you have had mercy on your fellow
servant just as I had on you?' "
MATTHEW 18:33 NIV

*D*rip. Drip. Drip.

No one was around to hear it. The dripping kept dropping. And as the water ran through the pipes and down the drain and out into the world, the amount of the water bill kept going up and up. The unsuspecting homeowner had no inkling of the problem until the bill arrived in the mail, weeks later.

Thankfully, the utility company had a forgiveness program. One time, every year, they would allow a bill "adjustment." If the customer could explain that there was a problem that had been fixed, the company would change the amount of the bloated bill to a normal expense. The customer didn't have to be extra special, or especially nice, or excellent in any way. All they had to do was admit they had a problem.

Imagine now, if that same customer, after having hundreds of dollars taken off their bill, turned around and harassed their neighbor for not returning a borrowed hammer. Wouldn't make much sense, would it?

But sometimes we forget how much we have been forgiven. And we hold on to grace in a pitcher with an airtight seal, instead of pouring it out on others in the same generous way it has been poured out on us.

———◆———

Lord, forgive me when I'm stingy with grace. Help me be a leaky pitcher,
letting Your grace spill out onto everyone I know. Amen. —M.L.

Adopted

Long before he laid down earth's foundations, he had us in mind, had settled on us as the focus of his love, to be made whole and holy by his love. Long, long ago he decided to adopt us into his family through Jesus Christ. (What pleasure he took in planning this!) He wanted us to enter into the celebration of his lavish gift-giving by the hand of his beloved Son.

EPHESIANS 1:4–6 MSG

The mother hen didn't mind that the egg was a bit bigger than the rest. She sat on it and warmed it and nestled her feathers around it all the same. To her, it was her child. Something to be protected and treasured. Wanted.

And when the little creature came poking out through the shell, the mother hen didn't care that there was a bill instead of a beak, that the little thing's toes were webbed together, and that it was about twice the size as the rest of her offspring. She adopted the duckling into her family without hesitation.

How wonderful is our Father God who has adopted us graciously into His family! Isn't it amazing to think of the Creator taking pleasure in us? Isn't it out of this world to accept this lavish gift of grace through His Son, our Brother, Jesus Christ?

———◆———

Father God, I feel like throwing a party when I think about Your amazing love for me. How shall I celebrate today? I'll start by serving You. Amen. —M.L.

They Do Not Know

"Father, forgive them, for they do not know what they are doing."
LUKE 23:34 NIV

When Jesus arrived in Jerusalem, days before His crucifixion, He was welcomed into the city as a king. A crowd had gathered—some followers, some Pharisees, and probably others—and the disciples shouted out in joyful voices: "Blessed is the king who comes in the name of the Lord!" (Luke 19:38 NIV). They laid their cloaks down in the road, covering the dust and dirt of the city and creating a path of honor and glory for their teacher and friend.

And even then, Jesus wept over the city. Looking around at the crowd, he remarked, "If you, even you, had only known on this day what would bring you peace—but now it is hidden from your eyes" (v. 42).

After His arrest and trials, a crowd shouted again. But this time there was hatred and fear in their voices: "Crucify him! Crucify him!" (23:21). And His cloak and clothing were stripped away to cover the dust and dirt of our souls as He stepped into the path of suffering.

And once again, Jesus looked around, facing the crowd, filled no doubt with some who had praised His entry into the city days before and who perhaps were even now joining in with the shouts and insults. They just didn't know who it was before them. They couldn't see Him. But still, Jesus said, "Father, forgive them."

All-knowing God, forgive me when I do not know.
Help me to know You more. Amen. —M.L.

Standards

Therefore no one will be declared righteous in God's sight by the works
of the law; rather, through the law we become conscious of our sin.
ROMANS 3:20 NIV

he woman scanned the aisles, her eyes traveling slowly up and down the shelves. At times she stopped and folded her arms in concentration. At other times she reached out a hand and then drew it back with a sigh. At last she grabbed a bolt of cloth, examined it, and said cheerfully, "This is it!"

At the checkout counter the cashier raised her eyebrows. The woman noticed and held up a swatch, "I know—it's a hideous shade of green, but it's the perfect match for the chair I need to repair!"

Without that swatch, she never would have found the right cloth. And without some standard to go by, we'd never be able to know the right way to live, and to recognize when we were straying from that way. God's commands are a gift of grace to us—a picture of the lives He created us to live. Through looking into His law, we can see how well what we are doing and saying and thinking match up to His expectations. And through His law, He helps us be repaired and restored so we can live with Him.

Lord, thank You for Your law. Thank You for all the knowledge You
offer to help me live the life You designed for me. Amen. —M.L.

True Children

*"But I say, love your enemies! Pray for those who persecute you! In that way,
you will be acting as true children of your Father in heaven. For he gives
his sunlight to both the evil and the good, and he sends
rain on the just and the unjust alike."*

MATTHEW 5:44–45 NLT

*Y*ou knew it was wrong. But you *almost* couldn't help it. Every time you saw Miss Perfect trimming her prize-winning rose bushes with her exquisitely manicured hands in her picture-perfect yard, you just wished a little thunder cloud would plop itself on top of her 2.75 well-groomed acres and trash them to bits. You could just see the downpour melting her updo, the rivulets of water turning black on her cheeks as her mascara finally gave out.

She was just so irritating. She could make you feel like nothing in two seconds with a cool glance that took in your whole person—from your decidedly untrendy messy bun to the dingy flip-flops from two summers ago, revealing your naked, completely unvarnished toenails.

But God calls His children to do better than to give in to petty jealousies and even somewhat sinister daydreams. He calls us to love others just as He does. He gives His light to those who worship Him and those who curse His name. He refreshes those who give Him everything and those who take everything they can get.

———◆———

*Lord, You know my thoughts. Make me more like You. Help me to
love even those who drive me up the wall. Amen. —M.L.*

She Keeps Believing

"There is no Rock like our God."
1 SAMUEL 2:2 NIV

In the time in which Hannah lived, the main function of a woman was to bear children. If she couldn't provide children for her husband, she was considered somehow damaged.

Hannah had been suffering with this image of herself for years. And even though her husband loved her, she couldn't get over her grief—her pain from the lack of the one thing she felt she was created to do.

But year after year, this woman of grace kept believing. When she went up with her family to offer sacrifices, she would pray. And God remembered her—He gave her a son, Samuel. And even then, Hannah kept believing. She believed God would take care of her son. Can you imagine how hard it must have been for her to give up her only child? But as she had promised, the new mother dedicated her first infant boy to service to the Lord who remembered her. She handed her baby over to the priest, and she believed God would bless her offering. Indeed, God gave Hannah more sons and daughters, and Samuel grew to be one who spoke with God.

We can witness her faith and gratitude in her prayer: "My heart rejoices in the LORD. . . . There is no one holy like the LORD; there is no one besides you; there is no Rock like our God" (vv. 1–2).

———◆———

*God, help me to be like Hannah and to keep believing
even when I can't see Your plan. Amen. —M.L.*

Grace of God Within

But by the grace of God I am what I am, and his grace to me was not without effect. No, I worked harder than all of them—yet not I, but the grace of God that was with me.

1 CORINTHIANS 15:10 NIV

Have you ever had one of those knock-down, drag-you-to-the-ground kind of respiratory infections? The kind that makes you want to stay in bed for a month and wish you had a butler? The kind that makes you miss your mom and homemade chicken noodle soup? (Even if your mom never made soup—you still want it.)

But the world won't stop because you have a respiratory infection. So you go to the doctor and get the latest and best antibiotic and within a day you are up and moving and working and going. But you feel that it's not really you—it's that medicine working in you. Maybe that and five cups of coffee.

We can all be thankful that God's grace works better than any antibiotic. His grace allows us to get up and move in service and work on loving others and go do what needs to be done. His grace allows us to become what He made us to be—His.

Father God, I am nothing without You. I don't deserve Your grace, but I'm so thankful You've given it to me. Amen. —M.L.

Grace of Giving

But since you excel in everything—in faith, in speech, in knowledge,
in complete earnestness and in the love we have kindled in you—
see that you also excel in this grace of giving.

2 CORINTHIANS 8:7 NIV

The budget is tight. Really tight. So tight there are no more holes on the family belt. So when it comes time to figure out how much you can give to God, you might be wondering if it's okay to skip it, just this once. Or twice.

But when things are tight, give anyway. When things are going well, give more. When things are uncertain, go ahead and give. You get the picture.

Why? Because giving isn't about what you can or can't do. It's about what God has already done. You give as an act of acknowledging His grace. You give because He's given everything for you. You give because He'll bless your willingness to do so. Try it and see!

Paul told the Corinthians about the Macedonian churches—how "in the midst of a very severe trial, their overflowing joy and their extreme poverty welled up in rich generosity" (v. 2). That generosity didn't come from the Macedonians. It's not going to come from us. It only comes from the grace of God.

———◆———

Lord, You've been indescribably generous to me.
Help me to give more than I think I can. Amen. —M.L.

Alive!

But God is so rich in mercy, and he loved us so much, that even though we were dead because of our sins, he gave us life when he raised Christ from the dead. (It is only by God's grace that you have been saved!)

Ephesians 2:4–5 NLT

Wilted. Gray. Dried up. The poor little plant didn't stand a chance. It had been neglected and left out in the cold. It didn't seem possible that it could recover when so much of it seemed frozen and dead. It was like the life had been sucked right out of it, along with every bit of moisture.

But the owner put the plant out in the sun. She gave it a little water. And something started happening. The stem stiffened. The gray turned green. And if you looked closely, you could see a little leaf bud starting to emerge. New life!

Have you ever been at such a low place in your life that you felt dead in your sin? You were like that dried-up plant—neglected, bent over with the weight of past troubles, distanced from the source of nourishment. Maybe you are even at that spot right now. Don't give up! Come to God. He is rich in mercy. He will pour out grace on you. He will make you alive again! Don't worry, He's conquered death before.

Lord, thank You for giving me new life. Amen. —M.L.

Eternal Comfort

Now may our Lord Jesus Christ himself and God our Father,
who loved us and by his grace gave us eternal comfort and a wonderful hope,
comfort you and strengthen you in every good thing you do and say.
2 THESSALONIANS 2:16—17 NLT

*N*ever-ending bowls of macaroni and cheese. The longest, fluffiest blanket in the world. Millions of puppies. Unlimited refills of hot chocolate. Daily hugs.

What would eternal comfort look like to you?

Whatever we might dream of as comforting, it's certain the God of heaven has something better in mind for us. He has given us the wonderful hope of living forever in the light of His love, the promise of forever peace, the freedom from sorrow, suffering, and death. Knowing all this, we can trust that the God of heaven can truly comfort us and strengthen us for anything we might encounter here on earth.

We can face bad days and know that they are temporary. We can deal with financial struggles and know that He will provide. We can make it through physical challenges and know He can bring healing. We can be treated harshly and answer with kindness. We can meet difficult people and realize they might need comfort too.

God of eternal comfort, strengthen me for whatever I need to say or do.
And help me to share Your comfort with everyone I meet. Amen. —M.L.

It Takes Practice

When God's people are in need, be ready to help them.
Always be eager to practice hospitality.
ROMANS 12:13 NLT

*I*f you want to be an expert at something, no matter what it is, it's going to take work. Even people with extraordinary gifts have to train to learn how to harness their talents.

Hospitality is not an exercise that comes easily for many of us. Maybe we never took the cake-baking and tea-making class. Maybe we feel like people will judge us for what we have (or don't have) to offer. Maybe we never learned small talk.

But God never says we have to be the hostess with the most-est to serve Him. Paul tells us to "be ready to help." He tells us to "always be eager." What do we do to be ready? Be available. That means we might need to keep some extra supplies on hand. Or maybe we need to be flexible enough in our schedules to allow for godly appointments.

Being always eager might actually be the harder thing for some of us to achieve. But thankfully serving God doesn't require us to feel excited about it all the time. We just have to be willing. And then we have to practice. Practice being kind. Practice sharing what we have, no matter how little it seems. Practice making people in distress feel a bit of peace. Practice offering grace.

———————◆———————

God, sometimes I just don't feel equipped to offer hospitality to others.
Help me to practice sharing even when I don't feel able. Amen. —M.L.

Counting

H ow many bites of broccoli do I have to eat?" "How much farther?" "How many more days till my birthday?" "How many more minutes do I have to practice?"

Kids sometimes seem obsessed with counting. They are figuring out how things work, and they don't have a good concept of how long it takes to get from A to B or to complete certain tasks. So they ask for a lot of measurements—how long, how much, how many.

Peter sounds kind of like a little kid when he asks Jesus about forgiving. He wants a limit—some standard that will tell him when he's done enough, when he's hit the mark. And as usual, Jesus doesn't exactly give the answer Peter was wanting to hear.

Seventy-seven. Jesus wasn't expecting us to count exactly to that number. He knew no one would really do that. Instead, He was saying we should keep on forgiving, again and again, in the same way that our God keeps on forgiving us. Even though we don't deserve it. Even though we keep doing the same wrong things. Even when we don't even realize what we've done. God keeps on pouring out His grace on us, no matter what.

Lord, I don't understand why You love us so much, but I'm glad You do. Thank You for forgiving me. Help me to be like You in forgiving others. Amen. —M.L.

Kind Words

Anxiety weighs down the heart, but a kind word cheers it up.
PROVERBS 12:25 NIV

Words carry such power. They have the power to heal or to wound, to strengthen or to scare, to empower or to emasculate, to care for or to cut off.

When someone is down, the worries of the world can fall on their shoulders. They seem to pile up, making many mountains out of the tiniest of molehills. Everything looks hard. All the endings seem like they will be sad ones. Solutions seem out of reach.

But a kind word can make such a difference. Asking a question about something of interest. Speaking a true word of praise for an accomplishment. Scheduling an appointment for time together. Dropping a simple compliment. Offering to do an errand. Surprising someone with a meal, a little gift, or a bunch of flowers.

Sometimes, we let trivial concerns block our kindness. *Maybe someone has already done that for them,* we might think. *Will they think I'm weird if I say that?* Sometimes, we just let our busy schedules overrule opportunities to be kind. *I just don't have time!*

But saying a kind word—either through text or by phone or in an email or in a card or in person—takes just a few seconds. And everyone should make time to lift just a little bit of a burden off someone's heart.

———————◆———————

Lord, thank You for the kindness You show me every day.
Help me to speak kind words to others. Amen. —M.L.

Inner Beauty

What matters is not your outer appearance—the styling of your hair,
the jewelry you wear, the cut of your clothes—but your inner disposition.
Cultivate inner beauty, the gentle, gracious kind that God delights in.
1 PETER 3:3–4 MSG

*A*re you a sweatshirt princess or the queen of couture? Do you get up in the morning and throw on whatever you find first or do you spend hours putting your look together? Peter says it doesn't really matter—at least, not to God.

It's not that it's a bad thing to care about how you look. And at times it is respectful and right to put on your best face, so to speak. But if you have the trendiest hair, wear jewelry with the biggest statement, and choose apparel from the most refined designers, none of that can make you beautiful if your spirit isn't right.

You've probably met people like this. They are the picture of perfection—right up until the moment they open their mouths. Then the foul language, insensitive talk, worthless whining, or crass conversation erupts, and that picture gets painted with a coat of ugly.

Work on your inner look. Cultivate kind thoughts, generosity, and peace. Train your mind to think on things that are noble and true and worthy. Remind yourself to see the good instead of the worst in others. Pray and ask God to shape your heart into one that delights Him with its beauty.

God, I want to delight You. Give me the grace
of inner beauty. Amen. —M.L.

Heat Relief

For day and night your hand was heavy on me;
my strength was sapped as in the heat of summer.
PSALM 32:4 NIV

Thick air lies like a heavy, damp blanket over the too-bright world. Even breathing makes you sweat. You find a tiny bit of shade and sit, aware of every ounce of clothing that is sticking to your flesh, and wish there was a nice, cool pool somewhere nearby to jump into. But you'll have to be satisfied with a glass of iced tea instead.

Have you ever experienced one of those long, hot, humid summer days? The kind that makes you praise God for the people who invented air-conditioning?

David compared enduring the heat of summer to how he felt under the weight of unconfessed sin. Have you known that kind of heat? The kind that comes from holding on too long to secret thoughts and actions that you know in your heart are doing you no good?

David says, "Blessed is the one whose sin the LORD does not count against them and in whose spirit is no deceit" (v. 2). He says he acknowledged his sin and confessed his transgressions to the Lord, and God forgave David.

We can receive the cool relief of our God's forgiveness too—all we have to do is confess our sins to Him. Then we will find rest in the shade of His grace.

———◆———

Lord, I want to tell You everything.
Please forgive my sin. Amen. —M.L.

Songs of Praise

*Birds find nooks and crannies in your house, sparrows and swallows make nests
there. They lay their eggs and raise their young, singing their
songs in the place where we worship.*

PSALM 84:3–4 MSG

It's a glorious sound—as long as you aren't trying to sleep in. As soon as that first sliver of dawn glimmers on the horizon, the beautiful notes erupt. As the morning wears on and the sky becomes golden, more birds join in the chorus, until there are layers upon layers of birdsong, and it becomes quite difficult to hear the distinguishing notes.

How wonderful that we have a God who not only made our world look beautiful—He made it sound lovely too!

Do you ever wonder what the birds are singing about? The experts might say differently, but especially in the mornings, their songs sound like praise. Praise for the God of the dawn. Praise for another new day. Praise for warmth and food to eat and trees to nest in. Praise for flowers and berries and bugs and blue skies. Praise for the limitless genius of the great Creator. Praise for the beauty and strength and power of the living God.

---

*Lord, my heart and my flesh cry out for You. Let my song of praise
and worship be as beautiful to You as the birdsong
is to my ears. Amen. —M.L.*

No More Stone

There was a violent earthquake, for an angel of the Lord came down from heaven and, going to the tomb, rolled back the stone and sat on it.
MATTHEW 28:2 NIV

One wonders if this messenger of God was trying to drive home the point. "Yes, it's over. Death has been defeated. It's all so over that I'm just going to take a seat, right here on the tombstone, and watch how you all deal with it."

The guards who saw this angel certainly couldn't deal with it. They fainted dead away in fear! But the women remained standing. They listened to the angel's words: "He is not here; he has risen, just as he said. Come and see the place where he lay" (v. 6).

The women ran off with the appropriate response—"afraid yet filled with joy" (v. 8)—and went immediately to tell the disciples.

Afraid. When we are met with the reality that there is a supernatural world we know nothing about, that there are beings created to deliver messages straight from the mouth of God, and that they glow with light we've never known, shouldn't it strike a little fear in our hearts?

And when we realize the stone—the weight of our sin and shame, the obstacle to our relationship with our living, loving Lord—has been rolled away like nothing and made into the seat of an angel, shouldn't our hearts be filled with joy?

Jesus, I'm so glad there's no more stone.
I praise my risen Savior! Amen. —M.L.

Willing Work

Work willingly at whatever you do, as though you were
working for the Lord rather than for people.
COLOSSIANS 3:23 NLT

*E*veryone encounters days of drudgery, when the hours are long and the minutes drag on and the work just doesn't seem to be worth it. But what if we changed our perspective? What if we filed papers, or computed accounts, or cleaned toilets as if we were doing it for our most holy, almighty, all-loving, God? The same God who came down into our dirt and was laid in a livestock feeding trough. The same God who squatted down in our dust and taught lessons with some writing in the sand. The same God who carefully cleaned the gunk off the feet of His friends. The same God who bore our sins on His back and suffered and bled and died—all for us.

Will the work get easier? Will the hours be shorter? Probably not. But the change in our attitude could change others. As they see us working with willing hearts, and not complaining, they'll wonder why. They'll wonder what makes us different from other workers. They'll wonder where our joy and spirit come from. And we might get the chance to tell them.

Lord, mold in me a willing heart—ready to do
whatever I can for You. Amen. —M.L.

In Which We Now Stand

Therefore, since we have been justified through faith, we have peace
with God through our Lord Jesus Christ, through whom we have
gained access by faith into this grace in which we now
stand. And we boast in the hope of the glory of God.

ROMANS 5:1–2 NIV

*H*ave you ever been put on the list for free entry to some special, exclusive event? Imagine the confidence that comes with the knowledge that you don't even have to hold on to a ticket—you can just walk straight up to the doorway, announce yourself, and you will be allowed in.

This is the same confidence and peace that comes through accepting the saving grace of Jesus. This grace gives us solid ground to stand on. We don't have to worry about losing our place. We don't have to hold on to a ticket. We don't have to pay for anything. We don't have to satisfy a dress code. We don't have to be with the right people. We don't have to bribe anyone. We don't have to flatter or flirt or be otherwise fake.

In this grace in which we now stand, we have gained access to the special, yet all-inclusive, love of Christ. And we can't ever be denied that. We won't ever be turned away. We will never be rejected.

And so, with every good reason, we can go out and most definitely "boast in the hope of the glory of God"!

———◆———

Thank You for Your amazing grace, Lord!
I'm so proud to stand in it today! Amen. —M.L.

The Struggle

For I know that good itself does not dwell in me,
that is, in my sinful nature.
ROMANS 7:18 NIV

Watching a small child trying to resist temptation is like watching a battle play out before your eyes. Set a toddler within reach of a glass of water, a flowerpot, a bag of candy, or any other desirable thing, and tell them to "not touch." Then sit in a corner and see the different phases of the struggle pass over their sweet little faces—sometimes all in a matter of seconds (toddlers are fast!).

At first, they get closer to the object. Their eyes widen with curiosity. Then they get close enough to touch. And often they will look around for the parent in the room as they reach out their little fingers, ready to grasp the very interesting item—made even more interesting by the warning.

Goodness, by itself, does not dwell in us. We have to have the Holy Spirit in us to help us be good. Without Him the battle is impossible to win. But even with Him, we still have to struggle. We are human, not divine. We can know goodness. We can practice goodness. But we have no goodness in us apart from God.

That's why we need to read His Word every day. Spend time with Him. Because the closer we get to Him, the easier the struggle becomes.

Lord, I want to do good, but it's so hard sometimes!
Remind me every day, Lord, to stay close to You. Amen. —M.L.

The Patience You Need

*We also pray that you will be strengthened with all his glorious power
so you will have all the endurance and patience you need.*

COLOSSIANS 1:11 NLT

The wait on the phone for the health insurance representative to answer. The line to get your license renewed. The days that pass before your tax refund comes. The hours before the doctor tells you how the surgery went. The minutes before your child replies to the text to tell you they made it safely to their destination.

All kinds of levels of patience are required from us on a daily basis. Sometimes, even waiting for the toast to pop up or for the coffee to brew seems like an eternity. Maybe you can't even make it through this page!

God knows our hearts. He knows the anxiety that preys on us. He knows our every worry and concern. And He has the power to give us patience and strength to make it through any journey and any delay. He knows exactly what we need to wait with grace. All we have to do is remember to lean on Him.

---

*Lord, sometimes I get so impatient, even when waiting for the smallest
of things. Lord, help me to feel Your presence with me. Help me
to depend on You for my strength and peace. Amen. —M.L.*

Holy Lives

God has called us to live holy lives, not impure lives. Therefore, anyone who
refuses to live by these rules is not disobeying human teaching
but is rejecting God, who gives his Holy Spirit to you.
1 THESSALONIANS 4:7–8 NLT

*S*ometimes you can detect a note of sarcasm in the writing of Paul. Here, as he reminds the Thessalonians to stay away from sexual sin, control their bodies, and not harm or cheat one another in their relationships, he makes a blatantly obvious point: "God has called us to live holy lives, not impure lives."

God does not call us to lie just a little. He does not call us to gossip just on Tuesdays. He does not call us to lust every now and then. He does not call us to be mean and hateful once a month. He does not call us to mostly be kind. He does not call us to sometimes think of others before ourselves.

He calls us to be holy. To be holy as He is holy. Set apart. Unique. Different from the world.

We can't do it on our own. We can never be perfect without Him. But with Him, ever and only with God, as amazing and difficult and frightening as it sometimes may seem, we can live holy, pure lives. It's a promise.

———◆———

Lord, make my heart want to be holy more
than anything else. Amen. —M.L.

For Us

If God is for us, who can be against us? He who did not spare his own Son,
but gave him up for us all—how will he not also, along with
him, graciously give us all things?
ROMANS 8:31–32 NIV

We work hard to get through school, to get a good job, to make money, to make a family, to feed our children—all so they can work hard to get through school, to get a good job, to make money. . .and so on.

But with all that working comes a kind of self-deceit. We think we're in control. We have to figure out how to solve our problems. We have to pay for our debts. We have to make things right.

But what if we can't? What if we can't do it all, make it all, fix it all? And what if we can? If we do all the right things to make a good life in this world, and yet have forgotten God, what will we really have?

God is for us. He wants us to live well. But living well in His sight may not look like anything that's on a magazine cover. When we depend on Him, trust Him, look to Him, He will graciously provide everything we need not just to make it through this life, but to be a blessing to others along the way.

---◆---

Lord, thank You for being for me. Amen. —M.L.

Do They Know Your Chains?

For everyone here, including the whole palace guard,
knows that I am in chains because of Christ.
PHILIPPIANS 1:13 NLT

*M*aybe you don't get asked to go to certain social functions. Maybe people don't include you in their secret jokes. Maybe you don't go to certain movies or read certain books. Maybe you aren't up on the latest television show drama. Maybe you get treated differently, for better or for worse, in any number of ways.

There are consequences for living in the grace of God. Living a life set apart for Him can be difficult in this world. It comes with its own set of challenges and mysteries and frustrations.

For Paul, living for the Gospel meant sometimes being imprisoned. Yet he assured his friends, the Philippians, that even prison was helping him spread the good news of Jesus Christ. Because even in prison, he could tell why he was there. He could tell all the guards and the visitors and the other inmates about the love of Jesus.

Do the people around you see your chains for Christ? Do they know why you live differently? If not, why not tell them today?

◆

Lord, make me bold and ever faithful, like Paul. Let me not be ever
ashamed of speaking about the love of Jesus. Amen. —M.L.

Generous Plans

But generous people plan to do what is generous,
and they stand firm in their generosity.
ISAIAH 32:8 NLT

*N*o one knew much about the man, which was unusual in the small town—he kept to himself much of the time. But rumors had spread about the masses of wealth the man had acquired over many decades of hard work.

And after his passing, the rumors turned out to be true. The man left money in his will to several benevolent organizations in the town—in fact, he had planned carefully and made sure to give every last cent away to people in need.

Although opportunities to be generous may arise all of a sudden—a family loses their house in a fire, a child drops his ice cream cone, the lady in front of you at the grocery store comes up short by a few dollars—the ability to be generous, and the willingness to do so, often take some planning and practice.

We have a great example set before us in the form of our Father God—who from before the creation of the world planned to do what was necessary to love us and to make us able to live with Him. And every day He practices His generosity by supplying all the encouragement and hope and strength and patience and other provisions—everything we need.

—◆—

Lord, help me to plan to have a generous heart,
empowered by Your grace. Amen. —M.L.

Paid in Full

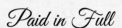

He has paid a full ransom for his people. He has guaranteed his covenant
with them forever. What a holy, awe-inspiring name he has!
PSALM 111:9 NLT

*P*aid in full." Are there any more beautiful words in the world than
those—especially when you've been in debt for a long, long time?

Some of you no doubt even now are longing to see those words. You've
been diligently working and making payments bit by bit, and yet still some
debt is hanging over you. That debt makes its mark on your life—guiding your
financial decisions, curbing your impulses, and causing all kinds of stress and
anxiety. That debt might keep you from going on much-needed vacations or
make you grieve over all the gifts you've been unable to give. It might make
you have to pass on amazing opportunities.

We can be thankful that there is no such debt hanging over our heads
as we think about the opportunity to live forever with our Lord. We don't
have to worry about getting in to heaven—He has paid our way already and
guaranteed our free access.

When we get to Judgment Day and our accounts are laid open, we'll see
those blessed words written over it all: "Paid in full."

———◆———

Lord, I don't understand how You can just forgive all the terrible
things I've said and done. But I believe Your death is enough
to cover us all. And I rejoice in that! Amen. —M.L.

Bloom

The desert and the parched land will be glad; the wilderness will rejoice
and blossom. Like the crocus, it will burst into bloom;
it will rejoice greatly and shout for joy.

ISAIAH 35:1–2 NIV

*B*efore these verses in Isaiah, the prophet was speaking of a time of God's judgment. It is described as a terrifying time when God would destroy all the nations who disobeyed Him—"all the stars in the sky will be dissolved and the heavens rolled up like a scroll" (34:4). It is a time of darkness and death, a "day of vengeance" (v. 8).

But in Isaiah 35 we read of a time of redemption, when all those saved by God see the glory and splendor of the Lord. They get to rejoice in the healing, renewing, strengthening grace of God.

Perhaps your life feels a little bit like a desert just now—hopes and dreams that you once had have dried up. Things haven't quite turned out the way you thought they would. Opportunities seem out of reach. And your spirit feels weak and wilted—like flowers in the heat of a too-bright sun.

Find your joy in the Lord. Get your refreshment from His Word. He has so much to offer you! His redemptive Spirit will show you the way to new, green paths filled with His plans. Your desert can be watered and bloom again!

———————◆———————

Lord, some days I just feel so tired and dried up.
Help me to find sweet refreshment in You. Amen. —M.L.

Asking for Wisdom

If any of you lacks wisdom, you should ask God, who gives generously to all without finding fault, and it will be given to you.

JAMES 1:5 NIV

*H*e knows the measurements of the mountains. He knows every star by name. He knows the number of the hairs on your head. He knows the weight of the oceans. He knows the thoughts of all the best minds that have ever lived or ever will live on this planet. He understands eternity and sets a bit of it in our hearts. He knows the sinful thoughts we had before we were even able to do anything about them. He knows the pain we bear.

And still, if we want wisdom, all we have to do is ask Him, and He will give it to us—all of us. Without finding fault. Without judgment. Without requiring something from us first. Without ridiculing us in our ignorance.

One wonders why we ever hesitate to come to Him, and yet we do. We try to find our own answers. We perplex ourselves with our own puzzles. We worry ourselves into frazzles. And yet He still waits for us. And all we have to do is ask.

God, I don't know why I sometimes seek wisdom elsewhere. Forgive me. Help me remember to ask You first. Amen. —M.L.

The Covenant

"Whenever the rainbow appears in the clouds, I will see it and remember the everlasting covenant between God and all living creatures of every kind on the earth."
GENESIS 9:16 NIV

Sometimes we forget that this whole story of our world could have ended very differently. God didn't have to start it all over again. People were wicked—that much was clear. When given the choice between obedience or rebellion, the majority would choose rebellion. Faced with the destructive forces of His creations, God decided to wipe every person off the face of the earth. And He could have just ended it there. He could have destroyed every person and left the world to the monkeys and the birds and the bugs.

But He didn't. We may never really understand the thinking of God, but for some reason He decided to give us another chance. He gave Noah and his family another chance. He spared their lives. Not only that, He encouraged them to be fruitful and multiply and fill the earth again with people. Even though He knew we'd be filled with trouble. Even though He knew we'd be wicked. Even though He knew we'd reject Him. He let us have another chance anyway.

Some might call that crazy. Some might call it crazy love.

And He made this covenant with Noah, and with all of us. Never again would He destroy the whole world. Instead, He would remember. He would remember He loved us.

God, Your grace simply amazes me.
I don't understand it. But I love You! Amen. —M.L.

Opportunities

The midwives, however, feared God and did not do what the king
of Egypt had told them to do; they let the boys live.

EXODUS 1:17 NIV

The king of Egypt was filled with fear. The Israelites were multiplying—even in their poverty, they were growing. And the king feared there would be an uprising. So he hatched a wicked population-control plan—kill all the baby boys. He gave specific instructions to the Hebrew midwives, Shiphrah and Puah: "If you see that the baby is a boy, kill him; but if it is a girl, let her live" (v. 16).

But he didn't count on one thing—the fear of God. And that fear, that reverence for the Creator, for the One True God of Israel, gave these women the strength to offer grace—even at risk of losing their own lives.

You never know when you might have an opportunity to offer grace. It may come at a time of blessing in your own life. It may come at a time of grief and pain. It may come when you are ready. Or it may take you by surprise.

Let the reverence you have for God give you the strength and courage to step out and offer grace whenever you have the chance. And God will bless you for your efforts.

———◆———

Lord, even when I'm scared of what might come next,
help me to offer grace when the opportunity arises. Amen. —M.L.

Everything We Need

By his divine power, God has given us everything we need for living a godly life.
We have received all of this by coming to know him, the one who called
us to himself by means of his marvelous glory and excellence.

2 PETER 1:3 NLT

"Batteries not included." The new remote-controlled car just wasn't going to work. No matter how much the little boy pushed it, or how hard he squeezed the buttons on the controller, the car wouldn't do what it was supposed to do.

Then we saw the notice printed there on the box, and we knew the reason for the malfunction. No batteries, no go. A quick trip to the store remedied the problem, and the boy enjoyed the car for the rest of the afternoon.

God has given us everything we need to go and live a godly life. He supplies the fuel that keeps us going. And we don't even have to make a trip to the store. We receive His power through knowing Him. He shows us His glory and excellence, and we can't help being drawn to Him. It's almost like He's giving out free batteries!

Lord, I'm overwhelmed with gratitude for how You've shared
a little bit of Your power with me. Thank You for supplying
everything I need to live a godly life. Amen. —M.L.

No Excuse

For ever since the world was created, people have seen the earth and sky.
Through everything God made, they can clearly see his invisible qualities—
his eternal power and divine nature. So they have no excuse for not knowing God.
ROMANS 1:20 NLT

*I*f you've seen the dawn light sparkle through the crystal beads of dew on each blade of grass on a spring morning, you have no excuse. If you've watched the leaves be painted shades of crimson and gold, you have no excuse.

If you've ever noticed the wonders at work in a bee gathering nectar from a flower, you have no excuse. If you've seen the beauty rippling through the muscles of a running horse, you have no excuse.

If you've gotten lost in the pure blue of an autumn sky, you have no excuse. If you've shuddered at the surprising crash of a thunderstorm, you have no excuse.

If you've marveled at the originality in each snowflake's design, you have no excuse. If you've listened to the might in the crash of ocean waves on a rocky shore, you have no excuse.

We can clearly see God's power and beauty and creativity and purity everywhere we look out in His creation. We can feel it all around us. We have no excuse for not knowing the source of our power and grace.

God, You are so amazing. I marvel at the
work of Your hands. Amen. —M.L.

Energy to the End

He is the one we proclaim, admonishing and teaching everyone with all wisdom, so that we may present everyone fully mature in Christ. To this end I strenuously contend with all the energy Christ so powerfully works in me.
COLOSSIANS 1:28–29 NIV

The car wouldn't go another inch. She had wished it. She had willed it. She had even tried to push it by moving back and forth in her seat. But it wasn't going to work. There was no doubt about it. The car was out of fuel. This wouldn't have been such a problem, but she was already running late. And now she would be running much, much later.

Do you ever run out of fuel? Maybe you think you have enough. You think you can manage everything in your schedule, and in the schedules of everyone in your family, along with all the surprise events that pop up naturally in the course of a week. But then just one too many problems arise, or one too many questions get asked, or one too many so-called easy solutions turn out to be more complicated.

Thanks to God, our energy to face the world can be replenished at a moment's notice. We don't have to get through this life on our own. His power works in us to give us words of praise and the energy to shout them; bits of wisdom and the patience to explain it; and supernatural self-control and the power to use it.

---◆---

God, thank You for using Your power within me! Amen. —M.L.

Nothing Better

I know that there is nothing better for people than to be
happy and to do good while they live.
ECCLESIASTES 3:12 NIV

*I*t sounds so simple. Be happy. Do good. Is that really all there is to life? Is that what God created us for?

And the answer is. . .yes.

Be happy. Be content with what you have. Don't spend time longing for what someone else has. Don't be greedy. Get rid of any feelings of entitlement you may be harboring. Be happy because you know that God in His grace has given you, and will continue to supply you with, everything you need to be a fully functioning human being.

Do good. Follow the example set by Jesus Christ. Be kind to other human beings. Share with those in need. Love people—not because of what they do for you, but simply because they are other creations of the Lord our God, and we are all in this together. And when people mess up, remember that you mess up too, and forgive them. Obey the commands of the Lord our God—love God and love others.

Now, the writer in Ecclesiastes does not say that there is nothing *easier* for people to do than to be happy and do good. Better does not mean safer, or able to be accomplished with less work, or easier to understand. Better just means. . .well, better.

Be happy. Do good.

———◆———

God, I know I can do good in this world as long
as You are with me. Amen. —M.L.

Awake

I stay awake through the night, thinking about your promise.
PSALM 119:148 NLT

There's a special stillness that comes in the middle of the night. A hush falls on the world. Birds stop singing. Cars stop roaming about. Even lights are put out.

The voices in your house are silenced. And in that quiet space, you can focus on the one voice that matters. You can read God's Word and hear the things He has been saying to His people for centuries—the promise He has given to never leave us or forsake us, but to instead prepare a place for us where we can live forever with Him.

And through His promise—through the grace He has given in order for us to be close to Him—we can have courage and strength and confidence to face the busyness of our day-to-day schedules. We can hang on to His words even when others speak harshly to us. We can hold on to the peace of His quiet even when the aggression and selfishness of the world gets so very loud.

Lord, sometimes I wake up in the night and the worries of this world crush me. I don't know what to do! Speak to me in the quiet and remind me of Your promises. Amen. —M.L.

Longing of the Lord

Yet the LORD longs to be gracious to you;
therefore he will rise up to show you compassion.
ISAIAH 30:18 NIV

The children watched the cake being made with eyes full of longing. Their noses followed the chocolate-covered spoon as it spun around and around, circling through the batter. They licked their lips, just waiting for the moment when they could have a lick of that sweetness.

Let's be truthful. Those kids didn't need the chocolate cake. They weren't starving. They weren't deprived. They just really, really wanted it.

It's stunning to think that the God of the universe—who has everything He could ever want or need—longs to be with us. He really, really wants to show us grace. He really, really wants to offer us compassion. Even when we've been terrible. Even when we've run the opposite direction from Him. Even when we're so unworthy. Even when we tell Him in a thousand ways that we don't need Him. God really, really wants to love us.

Do you know that? Will you accept His grace?

God, I'm amazed by the steadfast love You have for us. Your ability to
keep loving us even when we betray You just shocks me. But more than
that, the idea that You, God of all, want to be with me and long to
be gracious to me is simply incomprehensible. Help me to
be ready to receive Your grace. Amen. —M.L.

In Him

*In him and through faith in him we may approach God
with freedom and confidence.*
EPHESIANS 3:12 NIV

Grace has been described as not an emotion, but a location. Grace is a seat at the table. Grace is a ticket to the game. Grace is a place saved in the front row of God's mercy. Grace is a tent of meeting for the faithful. Grace is an *X* on the treasure map. Grace is a saved row in the cinema of our life stories. Grace is the seat of honor. Grace is our spot, right by the throne of God.

No one can make us leave. No one can throw us out. No one is allowed to harass us into giving it up. We cannot trade it. We don't get a refund for it. We either claim it, take it, and sit in it, or we deny it and lose it.

Sit down in your seat of grace. Accept the forgiveness of the Lord and Savior of all. Bask in the warmth and surety of His love. Approach Him with the freedom to speak the words of your heart and ask the questions of your soul. He will not turn you away. He will not make you wait. He will listen. And He will love you.

Your place of grace is here for you. Don't miss out on its glory.

*Lord, how can I ever repay You for this freedom to come to You?
I can't, but I will praise You all my life. Amen. —M.L.*

Let Us Run

*Therefore, since we are surrounded by such a great cloud of witnesses,
let us throw off everything that hinders and the sin that so easily
entangles. And let us run with perseverance the race marked out for us,
fixing our eyes on Jesus, the pioneer and perfecter of faith.*

HEBREWS 12:1–2 NIV

The key words found in this passage of scripture are little words: *we* and *us*. *We* are surrounded. Let *us* throw off. Let *us* run. Marked out for *us*. Fixing *our* eyes.

The Christian life was never meant to be a singular one. Throughout scripture, from the beginning of the world until the visions given in Revelation, we see that it is good for human beings to be together—to survive together, to decide together, to worship together. We are made to do life together. We are called to encourage one another, to challenge each other, and to love everyone.

Of course, sometimes it feels a lot easier to love people if you're not with them. But then again, that's not so much love as tolerance. And Jesus never said, "Tolerate each other's existence just as I have tolerated you."

As we work out what it means to live in the grace of God, let's remember to do it together.

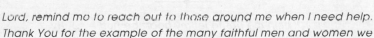

*Lord, remind me to reach out to those around me when I need help.
Thank You for the example of the many faithful men and women we
meet in the Bible, and for those in my real life right now. Amen. —M.I.*

In Your Anger

Therefore each of you must put off falsehood and speak truthfully to your
neighbor, for we are all members of one body. "In your anger do not sin":
Do not let the sun go down while you are still angry,
and do not give the devil a foothold.

EPHESIANS 4:25–27 NIV

*I*t started with a fence. When the fence went up, so did the blood pressures on both sides of it. There were arguments about the placement of the fence, the view the fence was blocking, the tree that touched the fence, and so forth and so on. Good fences might make good neighbors, as the old saying goes, but sometimes good fences just create good conflict points.

But when tempers get hot, sometimes words add steam. Sometimes truth goes out the window as we seek to exaggerate our opponent's offenses and paint a positive picture of ourselves. And sometimes we use words as weapons to inflict pain, open wounds, and deepen divisions.

It's not that the feeling of anger is wrong. It's natural, and sometimes people deliberately push our buttons. But anger can feed sinful action and lead to deceit, cultivating hatred.

We have to guard our hearts and remember that we've been given exceeding amounts of grace. We can extend that grace to others. Even over the fence.

---◆---

Lord, help me not to let my heart be hurt by petty
concerns and uncontrolled anger. Amen. —M.L.

She Gives All She Has

Jesus called his disciples to him and said, "I tell you the truth, this poor widow
has given more than all the others who are making contributions."
MARK 12:43 NLT

Maybe Jesus had met her before on one of His travels. Maybe He could perceive her situation from the look of her clothing and the little children grabbing at her ragged cloak. Or maybe He just *knew*, in the same way that the Son of God knew the woman at the well.

As Jesus watched the crowds who had come to the Temple to gather around the collection box, He noticed the rich people making grand displays—raining down their coins on the box so as to let everyone know how much they were contributing. But this poor woman came with little. She fumbled in the sack at her waist to find what she was looking for and then quietly dropped her two very small coins into the box. Perhaps she hurried away, pushing her children along in front of her, anxious to get away from the noisy crowds. Perhaps as she went, she offered up a murmured prayer—thanking God for supplying her with enough so that she could give some back to Him.

Having nothing, she gave it all to honor God. She gave 100 percent, instead of just the 10 percent that was normally suggested. This woman of grace gave it all because she knew she owed it all to God.

Lord, help me to give as generously and with as
willing a heart as this poor widow. Amen. —M.L.

Disciplines of Grace

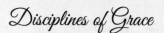

Endure hardship as discipline; God is treating you as his children.
HEBREWS 12:7 NIV

Stop! Hot! Don't touch! No! Bad!

When you are first training little ones, you have to keep things simple. They don't have huge vocabularies. They can't decipher complex commands. And they often move so very fast that you couldn't get out more words if you wanted to.

God keeps things simple with us too. "Endure hardship as discipline." What a different spin that puts on things! When we encounter difficult days, instead of blaming others or ourselves, we can consider it God's way of teaching us something for our good. Instead of asking, "Why me?" we can ask, "What lesson do you have for me in this, Lord?" Instead of asking, "Why now?" we can think about what has gone before or what might be coming in the future, and we can consider how the lessons we are learning currently might offer some help to us down the road. We can be reminded to pay attention closely, to jot down notes in our journals, and remember the feelings we had and the way we worked through the problems.

Hardship can lead us to other disciplines too. We can be called to prayer—placing the struggle before our Lord. We can be encouraged to read God's Word, finding comfort in His promises.

—◆—

Lord, I feel privileged that You call me one of Your children.
Help me to endure hardship with grace. Amen. —M.L.

Just as Christ Did

Accept one another, then, just as Christ accepted you,
in order to bring praise to God.
ROMANS 15:7 NIV

With all of our mistakes. With all of our faults. In our mess. With holes in our socks and smelly feet. With flabby middles and jiggling thighs. With annoying laughs and whiny complaints. With our worst Monday mornings. In our moments of darkness. In our deep-down doubts. In depression. In manic whirls of thoughtless activity. Caught in our temptations. Wrestling with questions we can't answer. In our arrogance. In our pride. Stuck in our ruts. Rejected. Damaged. Sinners.

This is how Christ accepted us. And He didn't just let us in the door to stand around and be ignored. He opened up His heart, and enveloped us in His arms of love, and embraced every bit of who we are—all the parts we like and all the parts we hate about ourselves. This is how Christ accepted us.

And that is how we are to accept one another. No holding back. No shame. No blame. No requirements. Just love.

Can we do this? Can we really look past each other's flaws and find the grace to accept one another in the name and in the example of Christ? We can—but only through Him.

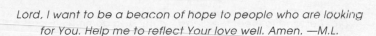

Lord, I want to be a beacon of hope to people who are looking for You. Help me to reflect Your love well. Amen. —M.L.

Learning to Do Good

"Learn to do good. Seek justice. Help the oppressed.
Defend the cause of orphans. Fight for the rights of widows."
ISAIAH 1:17 NLT

*I*n Bible times, and in many societies yet today, one's potential to earn an income is what determines one's worth. Those who can't earn—including children, those who are disabled, the elderly—are considered a drag on the rest of society. A weight that can't be shaken. A nonfunctioning part of the human race.

But in God's upside-down world, those who are least are considered the most valued. He points us in their direction first. He tells us we honor Him when we honor them.

And that is where doing good begins. We do good when we go out of our way to help those who have no voice. To offer ourselves in service to those who have no way to help themselves. To act as advocates for those who may have no fight left in them: orphans, widows, oppressed people.

What if you don't know any orphans or widows? Then you probably know some people who do. You can donate funds to help them. But also, look for who is the "least" in your environment. Who is being left out? Who gets the worst deals? Who gets nothing? Find those who need help and go show them what it means to be a child of grace.

Lord, help me to meet the "least" in my own community and
help me to reach out to them with humility and grace. Amen. —M.L.

Boast about This

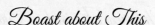

"Let not the wise boast of their wisdom or the strong boast of their strength or the rich boast of their riches, but let the one who boasts boast about this: that they have the understanding to know me, that I am the LORD, who exercises kindness, justice and righteousness on earth, for in these I delight," declares the LORD.
JEREMIAH 9:23–24 NIV

Maybe you've got five degrees in three languages from two different institutions. So what? God knows every tongue, tribe, and nation, and He communicates love in every language.

Maybe you've got the strength of an ox and have developed the ability to do more work in one day than most people can do in a month. So what? God measures oceans in His hands and carves mountains out of rock.

Maybe you've become the owner of ten companies and you make billions upon billions every year. So what? God owns your billions. He owns the cattle on a thousand hills, He owns the sun and the stars and the moon and the earth and everything in between.

But maybe you know the Lord. The Creator of the earth, the Almighty God, the Messiah, the God of heaven. Maybe you know Him well enough to have felt His kindness, experienced His justice, and gone after His righteousness.

Now *that's* something worth talking about.

———◆———

Lord, let my only boast be knowing You. Amen. —M.L.

Children Raised in Grace

Start children off on the way they should go,
and even when they are old they will not turn from it.
PROVERBS 22:6 NIV

*A*s new parents, we make mistakes. We forget a feeding. We hold the baby too much. We worry too much. We lose socks all the time. We forget to throw the dirty diapers out before they smell up the whole house. We don't get enough sleep. We cry. We yell. Oh dear—who's the baby now?

One thing we need to focus on as we raise our children is to teach them about God's gift of grace. We can teach them this in many ways—by reading Bible stories and talking to them about what Jesus did for us. But one of the most memorable, life-changing ways we can train our children in grace is by how we treat ourselves, each other, and them when we make mistakes.

"Don't cry over spilt milk," is an old saying, but there's truth in it. Don't make a big deal over the things that just don't really matter in the much bigger picture. When your child makes a mess, offer forgiveness quickly and fully. Give hugs often. Demonstrate and require respect. But live every day in grace. Then, as your children grow, they will become young ambassadors for the grace of the living God. And that's a beautiful thing.

———◆———

Lord, help me to raise my children with the same grace
You have given me as a child of God. Amen. —M.L.

The Humble

He guides the humble in what is right and teaches them his way.
Psalm 25:9 NIV

*D*o you ever wonder why there are so many stories about athletes who come from nothing—who start out as the smallest or weakest in their towns—and then become a model of excellence in their sport? Of course, we hear about these stories most often because they make good stories—we love the drama. But there are two reasons why people like this make it through the ranks and into the halls of history: (1) they have good coaches, and (2) they have nothing to lose.

When we are at our most humble moments, we are also at our most teachable moments. When we realize there is nowhere to go but up, we get a confidence that strangely is born out of weakness. We get a strength that comes from somewhere outside of us.

If we want to be models of righteousness and experts in grace, we have a great coach—the best, in fact. God will teach us everything we need to know. But if we want to become something really great in the kingdom of God, we have to start by getting really low. Get humble. He will lift you up.

———◆———

Lord, make me humble so I can look up to You. Amen. —M.L.

Crucified with Christ

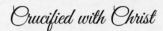

*Those who belong to Christ Jesus have nailed the passions and desires
of their sinful nature to his cross and crucified them there.*

GALATIANS 5:24 NLT

*I*n his letter to the Galatians, Paul is trying to encourage them to live as free people in Christ, and not to become hampered by traditions and behaviors that have nothing to do with being holy. He encourages them to leave behind the ways of their old lives and to focus on living by the power of the Holy Spirit instead.

He says the results of following the desires of our sinful natures are clear: "sexual immorality, impurity, lustful pleasures, idolatry, sorcery, hostility, quarreling, jealousy, outbursts of anger, selfish ambition, dissension, division, envy, drunkenness, wild parties, and other sins like these" (vv. 19–21). In other words—a lot of bad stuff for you and everyone around you.

These are the things we have to let go of. These are the things that must be nailed to the cross of Christ, and left with Him there. Only He can redeem us from lives filled and led by such desires.

Only He can take those desires and turn them into passion for the Spirit, who produces instead "love, joy, peace, patience, kindness, goodness, faithfulness, gentleness, and self-control" (vv. 22–23).

*Lord, I want to live by the Spirit. Help me to identify and get rid
of all those desires that are holding me back. Amen. —M.L.*

Still Sinners

But God demonstrates his own love for us in this:
While we were still sinners, Christ died for us.
ROMANS 5:8 NIV

When a couple finds out they are going to have a baby for the first time, they may feel extremely excited. They may even vent some of that excitement by preparing the baby's room. Before the baby's little legs and arms have even completely formed, they will go out and buy boots and jackets. Before the baby can smile, they make sure to have the best photo editing software in place. Before the baby can even see, they paint the room in pleasing colors.

They dream about what their baby will look like and sound like. They imagine making her laugh. They envision walking with her in a stroller, pushing her proudly down the street.

Before the baby is even fully shaped, they love her.

And that's how much God loves us too. He loves us so much, He sent His Son to die for us. Even though we were still sinners. Even though we were not fully formed into His disciples. Even though our lives were worthless, He redeemed us. Thank You, Lord!

———◆———

God, I will never understand how You looked into my heart
and saw something worth a place in heaven beside You.
But I'm so glad You've redeemed me! Amen. —M.L.

Sweet Healing

Gracious words are a honeycomb, sweet to the
soul and healing to the bones.
PROVERBS 16:24 NIV

Maybe you've had a rotten day. Maybe you missed your bus, and it rained, and your new boot got stuck in the mud. Maybe you had a headache to end all headaches at a conference meeting to end all conference meetings. Maybe your toddler vomited all over your tax paperwork. Maybe your husband lost his job, and you found out your grandma was sick on the same day.

Life can throw some horrible curves at us, can't it? You know what that's like. And you know what it's like when, in the middle of your mess, someone just compliments your hair, or tells you what a good job you've been doing, or encourages you that things will get better. Sometimes a few kind words can make you cry—but in a good way. You cry because you feel down in your bones that someone cares.

Remember that God always has a gracious word for you. And remember to offer gracious words to others, any chance you get. You never know when you might have just walked into someone's horrible curve. Help make it a little less horrible with a caring question, a kind compliment, or a meaningful moment.

———◆———

Lord, make me a blessing to someone today.
Give me gracious words. Amen. —M.L.

The Grace-Given Host

And when Jesus came to the place, He looked up and saw him, and said to him, "Zacchaeus, make haste and come down, for today I must stay at your house."

LUKE 19:5 NKJV

Sometimes all you have to do to offer grace to someone is to stand a little nearer to them. Jesus did this for Zacchaeus. Known as a tax collector and a cheat, Zacchaeus was not exactly a crowd favorite. When he wanted to see the teacher everyone was talking about, he knew he would have been squeezed out of sight behind the other people, so he climbed a tree to get a better look.

And Jesus, on His way to Jerusalem, where He would make the sacrifice for all of us sinners, looked straight at the wealthy man on the branch and made a statement to everyone in the area. Jesus not only included Zacchaeus, He honored him with His presence. "I must stay at your house."

The people didn't understand. Why would Jesus go stay with this sinner? But of course, they didn't understand that they were sinners too.

What Jesus did by getting closer to Zacchaeus had a life-changing effect on the man's heart. What you do when you get close to those who are abandoned, or shunned, or disliked may change their lives too.

———◆———

Lord, help me to reach out to those who are forgotten or ignored, and to those who are just plain awkward and irritating. Help me to share the love of Jesus with everyone on my way. Amen. —M.L.

Made New

You were taught, with regard to your former way of life, to put off your old self, which is being corrupted by its deceitful desires; to be made new in the attitude of your minds; and to put on the new self, created to be like God in true righteousness and holiness.

EPHESIANS 4:22–24 NIV

The old bike had seen better days. Its seat was squishy. The handlebars were bent in a way they were never meant to turn. The tires were flat. Rust caked the metal to such an extent, you couldn't even see what the original color was meant to be. It was all burnt orange now. The brakes didn't just squeak—they screamed.

But the boy set to work. He tightened up the brakes and made them safe and almost silent. He scrubbed off the rust with a wire brush until his own knuckles turned orange. He replaced and refilled the tires. He tightened up the screws on the handlebars and shined up the chrome. He bought a new seat and installed it on the bike. He worked and fixed and rubbed and cleaned until the whole bicycle looked brand-new. And it was as good as new. It functioned again, exactly as it was meant to do. The boy took off on a victory lap down the street, proud of his good work.

We have been made new. It's time we put down the scrub brush and start enjoying the freedom that comes with Christ. Let's put away our old behaviors and attitudes, and make sure we don't get rusty again.

Lord, thank You for making me new and putting the desire in my heart to be like You. Amen. —M.L.

Be Satisfied

Don't love money; be satisfied with what you have. For God has said,
"I will never fail you. I will never abandon you."
HEBREWS 13:5 NLT

It's interesting to note that some American money has on it the statement, "In God We Trust." Yet so many people put their trust in their bank accounts instead of in God.

But there's no banker that says to their customers, "I will never fail you."

Banks fail. Stocks fall. Accounts get compromised. Money gets taken. Bankruptcy happens. No matter how much money a person has, there is no true security in those funds. Millions can be made and lost again in minutes in our up-and-down, roller-coaster kind of world.

But we who trust in God can rest assured that He will never fail us. He will never leave us. And the God who can make those statements is the God in whom we can place our solid trust. We can believe that He will supply our needs. We can be satisfied with whatever we have today, knowing He holds all our tomorrows.

———◆———

My Father God, thank You for being my solid rock. Thank You for
making me feel safe and secure, no matter what my
bank statement says. Amen. —M.L.

Treasures

"For where your treasure is, there your heart will be also."
MATTHEW 6:21 NIV

We are sometimes so careless with our true treasures. We pay attention to where we put our money, and we carefully manage our accounts. But we let our promises be broken. We let gossip run through our mouths, jeopardizing reputations.

We take care of every detail of winterizing our cars and homes, making sure they are safe and prepared for harsh weather. We buy insurance and pay for it dutifully every month. But we let our Bible reading and our time with God be compromised. We slide into inaction when it comes to the disciplines of our faith. We don't take care to be sure our hearts are guarded and protected from the harsh attitudes of the world.

We put our most valued possessions away in locked boxes and combination safes. We hide them in secure locations. But we leave the Word of God lying around and forget to pick it up again. We let attitudes and selfish desires divide our family members. We let our hearts be stolen by the enemy.

Maybe today we need to take account of the things that really matter. Maybe we need to spend some time in the Word and in prayer to keep our hearts safe in Him.

Lord, I know what I value in reality doesn't match up with what is really valuable. Help me to get my priorities straight. Amen. —M.L.

His Peace

*"Peace I leave with you; my peace I give you. I do not give to you as the world
gives. Do not let your hearts be troubled and do not be afraid."*

JOHN 14:27 NIV

*H*ow does the world give peace? Temporarily. Conditionally. And
after much consideration. The world gives peace if certain rules
are followed. If certain systems are in balance. It gives peace that may last
only for as long as a treaty can be kept—which sometimes is a year, a month,
or even an afternoon.

The world gives peace that offers false promises of quiet and satisfaction.
It says that peace is all about you feeling good for the time being. Never mind
what happens tomorrow. Enjoy your moment now.

But Jesus offers us true peace. It's the peace that is beyond our
comprehension—it's that magnificent. And He gives it to us freely—with
no conditions. We don't have to sign a treaty or make any deals. We just have
to accept Him. He gives it to us forever. He gives us eternal peace through
the love and grace of our God.

The peace this world offers will not last. Trouble will come again. But
we don't have to be troubled by trouble. We don't have to be afraid of what
this world fears. We can hold on tight to the promises of Jesus and have true
peace in our hearts.

---

*Lord, I'm tired of being troubled and afraid. Help me to
understand the peace You have to offer. Amen. —M.I.*

Life through Him

God showed how much he loved us by sending his one and only Son
into the world so that we might have eternal life through him.

1 JOHN 4:9 NLT

*H*ave you ever put on color-tinted sunglasses? The world suddenly looks a little more yellow, or a shade of blue, or a little bit green. Maybe you've even looked through rose-colored lenses. The look of everything changes, and yet everything is still also the same.

When God sent His Son to die for us, everything changed about our world. Hope entered where it was not there before. Light shone into the darkness. Life defeated death.

But people are still the same. We still make mistakes. We still get sick. We still hurt each other. No one has become perfect. The way we have access to the hope and light and life is only through Jesus. Just like the way we can see in gold, or red, or green is only through tinted glasses.

That's the reason we need to stay close to Jesus. The closer we are to Him, the more we see the world through His eyes. The closer we are to Him, the better chance we have of walking in His light.

Lord, thank You for the gift of eternal life. Help me to stay close to You
and to remember to tell others about this gracious gift. Amen. —M.L.

No Other Name

*"There is salvation in no one else! God has given no other
name under heaven by which we must be saved."*

ACTS 4:12 NLT

*N*on-transferable. The ticket in her hand showed that word in big letters. That meant that it was good only for the person to whom the ticket had been assigned. She held tightly to the ticket as she entered the exclusive gala, showing her identification at the gate. Then finally, she was in. Safe. She breathed a sigh of relief—or at least, as big a breath as her tight evening gown would allow.

Our ticket to heaven has only one name on it. And it's non-transferable. No other name will get you in. Buddha won't work. Goddess Earth won't get you there. Nor Zeus nor Ra nor any other gods claimed by ancient or modern civilizations. But thankfully, Jesus has paid for us all to get in, and He's graciously given us all free access. All we have to do is get our tickets through Him.

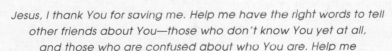

*Jesus, I thank You for saving me. Help me have the right words to tell
other friends about You—those who don't know You yet at all,
and those who are confused about who You are. Help me
make the path of salvation clear to them. Amen. —M.L.*

She Takes It All In

All who heard the shepherds' story were astonished, but Mary kept
all these things in her heart and thought about them often.

LUKE 2:18–19 NLT

*G*oodness gracious. Has there ever been any other mother in the history of the world who had more cause to make a commotion over her baby than Mary? Just think about it. People today give birth and put up Instagram posts and host parties and have banners and balloons and all kinds of celebrations.

Mary gave birth to the Son of God. The Son of God! If anyone had a right to crow about her birthing story, it would be Mary.

But she didn't do that. She watched. She listened. She looked. She saw a batch of strange shepherds come to her door and she heard the excitement in their voices. And she let them in and showed them her baby's shining face. And then she let them go and tell their story.

But Mary was a mom. And she had a new baby to take care of. And a new life ahead of her. And a promise from God. This baby, this son, would be the Savior of the world.

So Mary, in her moment of grace, took it all in, and remained quiet and humble in the sight of her God.

Lord, help me to remember not to be too quick to speak, but to take
time to understand what is happening around me. Help me
to let Your light shine, and not my own. Amen. —M.L.

Look Around

Do nothing out of selfish ambition or vain conceit. Rather, in humility value others above yourselves, not looking to your own interests but each of you to the interests of the others.

PHILIPPIANS 2:3–4 NIV

In any given day, most of us—as we go about running errands or commuting to work or taking kids to wherever they need to go—encounter several different people. Some might have familiar faces. Some might be imperfect strangers. Some might be having a good hair day. Some might have tripped in front of their bosses an hour ago.

You never know what people are dealing with. Everyone has a story. Most people have some kind of stress in their lives. Some have chronic illnesses. Others have financial struggles. Some are caught up in an emotional battle.

What can we do? We can offer grace. We can keep our eyes wide open. We can look around to detect those who are in need. We can be sensitive and compassionate, seeking to serve those who may be suffering. We can value others more than ourselves. We can look around, and we can notice everyone.

Lord, open my eyes. Lead me to those who need help.
Draw me to those who need Your love. Amen. —M.L.

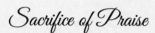

Sacrifice of Praise

Through Jesus, therefore, let us continually offer to God a sacrifice of praise—
the fruit of lips that openly profess his name. And do not forget to do good
and to share with others, for with such sacrifices God is pleased.
HEBREWS 13:15–16 NIV

You love that pie. It's your favorite—deep-dish apple cinnamon, with the best buttery, flaky crust in the world. You've been waiting to savor a scrap of that pie all day. So when you find out that someone else loves that kind of pie, and they're hungrier than you are, what do you do?

Eat the pie? Hmmm. Probably not the best answer.

God wants us to do good and to share with others, even when it hurts. In fact, if it doesn't hurt, at least a little, it's not really a sacrifice. God wants us to stretch and to give more than we think we can, because it's then that we realize how much we need Him, and how much He offers to us.

You will no doubt have times in your life when it's a sacrifice to offer praise to God. You may be ridiculed for attending worship services. Or you may have to choose whether to turn the Christian music up or down. But go ahead. Profess His name. And help others to know Him too.

---◆---

Lord, may the words of my mouth be a sacrifice
of praise to You. Amen. —M.L.

Blessing

May God be gracious to us and bless us and make his face shine on us—
so that your ways may be known on earth, your salvation among all nations.
PSALM 67:1–2 NIV

s there anything better than taking a walk with a friend on a sunny, warm day—when the smell of growth and new life is in the air? Each step leaves an imprint on your memories. Each moment with your friend, enjoying each other's company, brings you closer together. And when you have these blessed, golden moments, you always want more.

We are blessed to be a blessing. We are granted favor before God to offer favor to others. We are given His Word so we can spread His message. God has blessed us abundantly, and now is our time to honor that abundance by giving it away. We shall then want more and more and more. And we will give more and more and more away. We will offer an extra helping of grace and goodness and truth and compassion to everyone we meet. And by our blessings, all people will be blessed. And by shining on us, God will reflect His light into every corner of this dark world.

Lord, make me a blessing to others. Let my face radiate
the joy of Your light. Amen. —M.L.

Forgiving God

But you are a forgiving God, gracious and compassionate, slow to anger and abounding in love. Therefore you did not desert them.

NEHEMIAH 9:17 NIV

The Israelites had just finished rebuilding the wall of Jerusalem, establishing the boundaries of the holy city of God. Now they gathered together to confess their sins and to read from the book of the Law and to worship God as one body.

The Levites cried out with loud voices, calling the people to stand up and praise. Then they recited all the ways God had rescued His people, time and time again. They talked about how God created the heavens and the earth, and gave life to every person. They praised Him for calling Abraham to lead His people. They honored Him for answering the cry of their ancestors in Egypt and rescuing them by leading them through the Red Sea.

They spoke of how God delivered His commands to His people, but they did not obey. Instead they turned away from Him and failed to remember all that He had done for them. And even then, God did not desert His people. He forgave them. Time after time. He offered them grace.

If God, after all He did for His people, can forgive their betrayal and rebellion, who can we forgive today?

———✦———

Lord, You have set a high standard for forgiveness.
Help me to get better at forgiving others. Amen. —M.L.

Gift of Healing

Jesus went through all the towns and villages, teaching in their
synagogues, proclaiming the good news of the kingdom
and healing every disease and sickness.

MATTHEW 9:35 NIV

*I*t would have been enough that He came down to earth for us. That
the God of heaven appeared in a manger to live among us and care
about us—that would have been enough.

It would have been enough that He taught us. That He went from place to
place, teaching His disciples and training them to love God and love others. It
would have been enough that He shared a bit of His eternal wisdom with us.

It would have been enough that He established His kingdom on earth
and invited us to live in it. It would have been enough that He told us how
to live as citizens of this new kingdom.

It would have been enough that He suffered and bled and died for us.

But on top of all that, He made people feel better too. He healed their
bodies from disease and dysfunction. He made them whole, physically and
spiritually.

He didn't have to do that. It's not why He came. But He did it anyway.
That is our gracious, loving, compassionate God.

Lord Jesus, Your capacity to love and care for us amazes me.
Thank You for every miracle You performed. Help me
to know Your power. Amen. —M.L.

Level Land

Teach me how to live to please you, because you're my God. Lead me by your blessed Spirit into cleared and level pastureland.

PSALM 143:10 MSG

*S*oft grasses wave in the warm breeze. You reach out your hand and can easily grasp handfuls of blossoms. You walk without hindrance—the way is clear and smooth. No brambles claw at your clothing. No rocks are in your path. No bumps or lumps trip you up. You can see the path running out ahead of you for a long way, with no end in sight. You stroll along at a steady yet leisurely pace, admiring God's green earth.

This is the picture of walking with the Spirit. When we rely on His guidance, our way becomes easier. We can find security in trusting His Word because we know He knows the path ahead. He knows where we are going and the troubles that will come. He can give us everything we need to know to survive the journey and thrive in the end. When we follow God's commands, He promises to take care of us. He blesses our efforts and leads us to relief and rescue. He leads us to a place of peace—like a clear, level path through a beautiful pasture.

———◆———

Spirit, lead me, guide me, teach me, correct me.
Help me to follow You so I may know Your peace. Amen. —M.L.

Looking in the Wrong Places

As the crowd swelled, he took a fresh tack: "The mood of this age is all wrong.
Everybody's looking for proof, but you're looking for the wrong kind."
LUKE 11:29 MSG

*H*ave you ever asked God for a sign? Have you ever wished He would offer up a clear signal—perhaps make your television flash green for go or red for stop any time you were considering some options? You're not alone.

After all, the people Jesus was speaking to actually had the Son of God right there in front of them—the living, breathing, teaching Son of God. And yet they were still looking somewhere else. They were still wanting something that fit the picture in their heads.

We can do better. We can let go of our expectations about how God will speak to us, and instead dig into His Word. We can stop waiting for a sign and start listening to the Savior. We can stop looking in all the wrong places and follow what we know to be right.

We have all the proof we need in Jesus.

---◆---

Lord Jesus, I know You are the Way, the Truth, and the Life.
Thank You for coming and showing Yourself to us. Amen. —M.L.

Watching Over Me

*The LORD himself watches over you! The LORD stands beside
you as your protective shade.*
PSALM 121:5–6 NLT

Sometimes people think of God as a great big policeman in the sky,
watching us and waiting for us to mess things up. They think God delights
in our weakness and failure, and that He can't wait to bring punishment on
us. They might picture God as a demanding boss figure, shouting out orders
and sending people scrambling.

But they've got it all wrong.

The God we see in scripture delights in His relationship with us. He is
not waiting for us to mess up; He is watching out for us. He doesn't want to
punish us; He wants to protect us. He stands over us, offering shade in this hot
mess of a world. He takes the time and attention to care about what each of
us is doing and where we are going. He draws us closer to Him, instead of
pushing us away. He holds on to us tightly, instead of leaving us on our own.
He loves us!

*God, I'm so thankful that You aren't just waiting around for me to mess
things up. Thank You for protecting me from my own destruction.
Thank You for offering me kindness and grace. Amen. —M.L.*

Friend of Nobodies

Make friends with nobodies; don't be the great somebody.
Romans 12:16 msg

When we have been walking with the Lord for a while, and we're doing okay at it (not perfect, but you know, we're trying!), sometimes we might gain an extra passenger on our walk of faith. Who? Pride.

We can easily become proud of our righteousness—even when we know that righteousness is impossible without God. But we might get afflicted with the disease of "comparisonitis." That is, we compare ourselves to others around us and decide that we are better—for whatever reason. Maybe we pat ourselves on the back because we don't smoke, or we don't swear (that much), or we don't overeat, or we don't cheat on our taxes (even though we wish we could). Maybe we think we know more of God's Word, or we pray more, or we serve harder.

But whatever we are able to do or have become is all because of God. We have no right to think of ourselves as better than anyone else. And everyone falls short of the glory of God. So we shouldn't let our pride become our only friend for this journey through life. We should kick out pride and let others in—especially those we may think of as the least, or as nobodies in the kingdom of God. After all, Jesus was pretty keen on the "least of these."

---◆---

Lord, help me to realize that I am nobody without You. Amen. —M.L.

Don't Be a Liar

If someone says, "I love God," and hates his brother, he is a liar;
for he who does not love his brother whom he has seen,
how can he love God whom he has not seen?

1 JOHN 4:20 NKJV

Relationships can be messy here on this earth. It can be painfully difficult to get along with some people. At times we will be hurt by others—truly and deliberately hurt. There may be even some people in our lives who seem as though they wish us harm. They are out for revenge, perhaps, or just envious of us.

But even in the worst relationships, no person is all evil, all the time. We can find reasons to be patient. We can find motivation to be kind. We can look at people and realize that they may have suffered from pains and stresses that we know nothing about. We can forgive and give a second chance. We can demonstrate the grace of God.

If we can't do that—if we can't even try to love the people in front of our faces—then we may well struggle to truly love God. And that would be a real mess.

Lord, I'm thinking right now of a difficult person in my life.
Help me to love them. Amen. —M.L.

My Light

The LORD is my light and my salvation; whom shall I fear?
The LORD is the strength of my life; of whom shall I be afraid?
PSALM 27:1 NKJV

A rattle. A clank. A soft, scrabbling sound. Is it the wind? A squirrel on the roof? A tree branch scraping up against the side of the house?

In the dark, our minds can suddenly soar to new heights of imagination—creating monsters out of molehills. Tiny sounds become magnified into terrifying enemies. Mysterious noises find definitive categorizations in the library of horrors that exists in the middle of our brains. But flip on a bedside lamp and suddenly the monsters slink away. The horrors become much less horrible. The true source of the sounds gets revealed. And all is well again.

In the darkness of this world, it's very easy for us to listen to small voices and scrabbling souls and feel a little lost. We invent terrors and troubles in our minds. But when we focus on the light of the Lord, He gives us strength to face our fears—whether real or imagined.

And He doesn't even laugh at us for being a little scared.

————◆————

Lord, thank You for filling my life with light. You are my hope and my salvation. You are my strength, and I depend on You. Amen. —M.L.

Renewed

Therefore we do not lose heart. Though outwardly we are wasting away,
yet inwardly we are being renewed day by day.

2 CORINTHIANS 4:16–17 NIV

*I*s it time for a new you? A new hairdo, maybe, or a manicure? Maybe you need a new outfit or an exercise program. Or maybe what you need is to be inwardly renewed instead.

Paul gives his Corinthian friends a long list of ways in which he and the other disciples have been impacted by their commitment to follow Christ and preach the gospel: "We are hard pressed on every side, but not crushed; perplexed, but not in despair; persecuted, but not abandoned; struck down, but not destroyed" (vv. 8–9).

And then he goes on to explain how they view these troubles: "For our light and momentary troubles are achieving for us an eternal glory that far outweighs them all" (v. 17). He reminds the Corinthians to fix their eyes not on what they can see, but on the unseen, because "what is unseen is eternal" (v. 18).

How amazing that Paul can present a list of hardships that would make most of us cry, and then call it "light and momentary"! This is the beauty and the wonder of the grace of God that gives us the ability to see beyond what human eyes can see and refreshes our hearts and minds every day, when we come to Him.

Lord, renew me! This old body will crumble away, but please keep my mind and heart firmly standing in You. Amen. —M.L.

All You Have to Do

"Ask and it will be given to you; seek and you will find;
knock and the door will be opened to you."
MATTHEW 7:7 NIV

Are you longing for a closer relationship with God? Do you want to feel more as though Jesus were truly your friend and your support? Are you trying to find a way to navigate through a difficult situation? Are you wondering if there might be a new way to be challenged and guided to live a godly life?

All you have to do is ask. Seek. Knock.

Sometimes we make things too difficult. Does anyone want to say amen? Sometimes we create obstacles in our own paths. Sometimes we don't need another program or another incentive. What we need to do is simply trust God.

Think about all the times God has provided for you. Think about all the ways He has supported you and loved you. Write them down, if you want. Look at that list whenever you need to remember who you can go to for help. Look at it whenever your next steps seem clouded in doubt.

Ask. Seek. Knock. He will answer. He will give. He will reveal Himself. He will open the door.

Lord, I trust You with my life. Help me remember to trust You
with my everyday problems too. Amen.   M.L.

Go for Glory

A person's wisdom yields patience;
it is to one's glory to overlook an offense.
PROVERBS 19:11 NIV

*H*e cuts you off in the school pickup line as you are patiently waiting for your children. She grabs the last discounted ham away from your hands. Someone cheats you on the price of tickets and you find out too late to do anything about it.

Go for glory.

You hear that she's been talking behind your back and making false statements about you—again. In an irritable moment, he made an unkind remark that hurt your feelings. She snapped at you when you asked a simple question.

Go for glory.

They didn't think you could make it, and they told you so. They sabotaged your agenda and sent your meeting into chaos. When they could have chosen kindness, they chose sarcasm and an easy laugh instead.

Go for glory.

We may be faced with millions of moments when we have the opportunity to overlook offensive statements, actions, or attitudes. And in every one of those moments we also have the opportunity to reach for the glory that God alone can give.

Lord, already today I have been faced with irritating moments.
Help me to turn offenses into opportunities to
bring glory to You. Amen. —M.L.

Raising Holy Hands

Since prayer is at the bottom of all this, what I want mostly is for men to pray—not shaking angry fists at enemies but raising holy hands to God.
1 TIMOTHY 2:8 MSG

*D*oes it ever seem like the whole world has anger issues? National leaders pick at each other. Armies push each other into battles. Bombs are dropped to serve as warnings. Even companies sometimes get into the fray, with corporate leaders hurling insults at one another. Efforts at peace are often rejected and sometimes not even attempted.

Surely in our churches we can provide something different. We can be a place of peace. We can be a safe refuge. We can keep our heads together when problems arise.

But we often fail at that too. Church people sometimes get into fights over the most ridiculous things—from colors of carpet to types of seats. Everyone has an opinion. And everyone wants to shout about it. And everyone thinks they are right and everyone else is wrong.

Can you imagine what would happen if, in the middle of the next congregational meeting where tempers were rising, someone would just start praising God—lifting hands in holy praise of the Prince of Peace? It would be hard to argue with that.

Dear Lord, help me to be an instrument of Your peace in an angry world. Amen. —M.L.

A Woman of Grace Laughs

Sarah said, "God has brought me laughter,
and everyone who hears about this will laugh with me."
GENESIS 21:6 NIV

Imagine for a moment being old—really old. Well past your child-bearing years. Well past anyone's child-bearing years! Then imagine what it might feel like to have a messenger from God—not the doctor's office, but God!—tell you that you would surely give birth in the coming year.

Would you laugh? Or would you just cry?

Sarah laughed—not at God, but at the ridiculousness of her own situation. She knew it wasn't humanly possible for her to have a baby. But what she didn't expect was that God could work the impossible in her.

So when that baby boy was born, Sarah kept on laughing. But this time she wasn't laughing just at her own foolishness, she was laughing with delight at the marvelous, joyous, surprising grace of God. She was laughing at her own disbelief—because who wouldn't trust the God of all? She was laughing at the amazing joke played on her by a God who loves to do the unexpected and make us remember that we can never know His thoughts.

Lord, help me to be able to laugh at my own foolishness. And make
that laughter remind me always to trust Your plan, no matter how
little sense it makes to me at the time. Amen. —M.L.

Church

*But you have come to Mount Zion, to the city of the living God, the heavenly
Jerusalem. You have come to thousands upon thousands of angels in joyful assembly,
to the church of the firstborn, whose names are written in heaven. You have come
to God, the Judge of all, to the spirits of the righteous made perfect, to Jesus
the mediator of a new covenant, and to the sprinkled blood that
speaks a better word than the blood of Abel.*

HEBREWS 12:22–24 NIV

What does church mean to you? What makes for a good church service? Is it the singing and worship? Is it the preaching? What do you enjoy most? Is it the fellowship?

When we come together as believers, it's important to remember why we are there. And it's vital to remember who is there with us.

We come to meet God and worship Him as one body. We come, because where we are gathered in His name, He is there.

We come to the home of the living, all-powerful, all-knowing, all-seeing God. We come as thousands upon thousands have done before us through century upon century. We come, even as the angels do, gathering to praise and honor the God Most High. We come to rejoice. We come to confess. We come to ask. We come to encourage. We come to love. We come to accept the sacrifice of Jesus Christ.

---

*Lord, I want my praise to honor You. Help me take
seriously my part in the body of believers. Amen. —M.L.*

Eternal Pleasures

You make known to me the path of life; you will fill me with joy
in your presence, with eternal pleasures at your right hand.

PSALM 16:11 NIV

A back rub that goes on forever. Taking off winter boots after a long day and putting your feet by a cozy fire. Perfectly seasoned food made and cleaned up by someone other than you. The heavenly aroma of sweet spring blossoms wafting through the air on a gorgeous, warm, sunshiny day. The sparkling of sun-kissed ocean waves as the tide comes in. The sound of crickets greeting the moon.

What eternal pleasures might God have in store for us? Isn't it wonderful to know that He is preparing a place for us to live with Him—and that He intends it to be a place of never-ending joy for us?

On days when life is difficult—when your feet hurt and your head aches and stress sits heavily on your shoulders—close your eyes and remember that there is a place for you where joy and peace and security remain. There is a place for you where all the aches and pains will be taken away. There is a place for you with no stress and no worries. There is a place for you with God.

———◆———

Lord, thank You for the grace that allows me to
have hope in heaven. Amen. —M.L.

Graceful Exit

No temptation has overtaken you except what is common to mankind.
And God is faithful; he will not let you be tempted beyond what you
can bear. But when you are tempted, he will also provide a
way out so that you can endure it.

1 CORINTHIANS 10:13 NIV

The colorful, sprinkled, sugary donuts call out to you from the bakery window. You promised you wouldn't. The doctor told you that you had to watch your diet, and your family made you promise that you would. But those donuts—they're so lovely and yummy!

Or maybe you have a chance to get a little extra income this month. You can sign up for a paid study—but you'd have to lie about your experiences a little to be accepted. It would just be a little lie.

Maybe you are thinking about deceiving a friend. You want to go to a concert on the same night the friend is having a party. You don't want to hurt anyone's feelings. Wouldn't it be better to come up with an excuse so the friend doesn't feel bad?

Temptation comes in all kinds of sneaky, weasel-ish, downright dirty forms. Sometimes it's just too much for us to take on our own. Thankfully, we don't have to face temptation alone. If we look to God, He will provide us with a graceful exit.

Lord, help me to remember that You know my heart. And You know
my weaknesses. Help me deal with my temptations. Amen. —M.L.

Led by a Child

The wolf will live with the lamb, the leopard will lie down with the goat,
the calf and the lion and the yearling together; and a little child will lead them.
ISAIAH 11:6 NIV

Children are naturally trusting beings. Sadly, that's why parents have to work hard to train them not to talk to strangers. Children don't know enough yet about the world to know that some people have bad intentions. They don't know that some people say one thing and do something else.

In Isaiah 11, we get a glimpse of a vision of the world in a state of peace, where every creature and every person resides side by side with no struggle, no strife, no competition, and no desire to hurt one another. Wolf and lamb can play together. Leopard and goat can leap together. Calf and lion and yearling can all nap together.

And a little child, the master of trust, is leading them. Because when the earth is "filled with the knowledge of the LORD" (v. 9), all His creation will understand that trusting one another is the best way to live.

And maybe we can start trying to trust one another a little more even now. . . .

Lord, I love to think of a time when all of creation can live together in
unity—no killing, no dying, no destruction. Yes, Lord! Amen. —M.L.

As the Lord Forgave

Bear with each other and forgive one another if any of you has a grievance against someone. Forgive as the Lord forgave you.

<small>COLOSSIANS 3:13 NIV</small>

*H*ow does God forgive? Completely. Again and again. Openly. Unconditionally. Consistently. Graciously. Generously. Lovingly. Often. Before we even know to ask. And always without asking anything of us.

This is the model of forgiveness for us. Whenever someone does something we don't like or whenever someone either accidentally or purposefully tries to hurt us, we are challenged to forgive. And not to forgive in the way human beings often do—with strings attached, or lording it over someone. We should not forgive in a huff. We should not forgive dishonestly—saying we forgive but really going away and holding on to bitterness about the issue. We should not put conditions on our forgiveness ("I'll forgive you, as long as you. . .").

On the other hand, we are not God. We are not perfect. Forgiveness may not come easily to us. We may have to practice. A lot. And that's okay. We may also have times when, because of the nature of the offense (perhaps we could even be in danger), we may have to allow time and space before we are able to truly forgive. And we may have to wake up every day and decide to try to forgive again.

The important thing is to keep aiming for the goal—to forgive as the Lord has forgiven us.

Lord, I want to forgive like You do. Help me, please. Amen. —M.L.

My Shepherd

GOD, my shepherd! I don't need a thing. You have bedded me down in lush
meadows, you find me quiet pools to drink from. True to your word,
you let me catch my breath and send me in the right direction.

PSALM 23:1–3 MSG

*H*ow gracious is our God who takes good care of us, like the best shepherd does with his flock of sheep!

The shepherd watches out for all the creatures in his care. He knows they do not know all the dangers in their way. He knows they cannot always see the best way to go. He knows they don't always find the best places for nourishment. He has organized the schedule so they get the right amount of food at the right times, and so they have plenty of water to keep them well hydrated. He looks at all the details and thinks them through. He always has the best interests of the animals at the forefront of his mind.

In the same way, God is always watching out for us. He lets us choose our paths, but when we look to Him, He offers us wisdom and guidance. He helps us find the way that will lead to righteousness. He supplies us with everything we need.

What a relief to know that He is caring for us every day!

———◆———

Lord, thank You for being my good Shepherd. Amen. —M.L.

Grace to the End

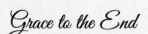

I have fought the good fight, I have finished the race, I have kept the faith.
2 TIMOTHY 4:7 NIV

Here lies a woman of grace. She kept the faith.

Have you considered what your tombstone might say? Have you thought about what legacy you will leave behind? Have you wondered what impact you are having on others around you?

Paul was secure in the way he had lived his life. He knew he had given everything he had to follow Christ and preach the Gospel. He knew that a "crown of righteousness" awaited him in heaven (v. 8). He knew that when the Lord, the righteous Judge, came to look at his life account, he would be found faithful. He was certain of his award.

How sure are you that you have fought the good fight? Have you been living for Jesus, or living more for yourself? Are you ready for the time when you will finish the race and meet the Lord face-to-face? If not, what can you do right now, today, to make a difference?

Lord, I know You offer me grace all the days of my life. I want to live in that grace to the very end of my time here on earth. I want to finish His race well. Help me see how to do that. Amen. —M.L.

Love Covers

Hatred stirs up conflict, but love covers over all wrongs.
PROVERBS 10:12 NIV

It begins with noticing differences. Little things that set us apart. The things that make us distinct. The things we don't do the same way. We notice these things, and that's just fine. Until someone decides one way is better than another. Then those little differences create a bigger rift. One group feels superior and wants to make the other group feel inferior. Before you know it, one group is trying to impose its ways on the other group. Then the shouting and the scuffling and the struggling starts. Someone gets hurt. Someone points the finger of blame. And the tensions of difference erupt into trouble. And this kind of trouble feeds the hatred that is present and easily accessible to every human soul.

But love covers. Love doesn't cover up—no, it does not hide the pain and the wounds and the torment. But it covers. It brings all the shouting voices under one tent of peace and helps us find our way to harmony again. Love covers. Like a bandage on an open sore, love protects and creates an environment for healing. Love covers. It pays the debts; it makes things right again; it redeems. Love covers over all.

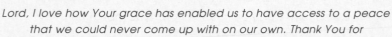

Lord, I love how Your grace has enabled us to have access to a peace that we could never come up with on our own. Thank You for loving us so much. Help us to love like You. Amen. —M.L.

See to It

*Make every effort to live in peace with everyone and to be holy; without holiness
no one will see the Lord. See to it that no one falls short of the grace of God
and that no bitter root grows up to cause trouble and defile many.*

HEBREWS 12:14–15 NIV

See to it. It's a command, not a suggestion. It's an intentional act to be done right now, not a maybe-someday kind of wish.

See to it. Don't just make half-hearted attempts at living in peace with your brothers and sisters in this world. See to it. Don't expect someone else to make the first move, to take the first step, to say the first "I'm sorry."

See to it. Don't assume people know the truth. Make sure they know it. Make sure they are being taught from the Word of God. See to it. Don't wait for someone else to take responsibility for your community. See to it. Don't let others fall short of the grace of God without trying your level best to get them on the right path. See to it. Don't let your friends stumble. Clear the way.

See to it. Don't let bitterness take root in your life or in the lives of others. Pull out the source of the bitterness and cut it up and get rid of it. See to it. Don't let selfish desires sabotage anyone's attempt to follow the will of God. Speak godly truth to people. Set people straight. Turn them back to the Lord.

See to it.

———◆———

Lord, help me to see to it! Amen. —M.L.

She Is Ready to Worship

*Then Miriam the prophet, Aaron's sister, took a tambourine
and led all the women as they played their tambourines and danced.*
EXODUS 15:20 NLT

he Israelites had packed up and left Egypt in a hurry. When it finally came time to get out of the land of their suffering, they made haste. They were moving so fast, they didn't even take time to wait to add yeast to their bread dough. They wanted to get out of there before Pharaoh changed his mind—again.

But here, after the crossing of the Red Sea, after the Lord had vanquished their enemies the Egyptians in the waters of the sea, we notice that the Israelite women took the time to bring one more thing along with them. Their tambourines.

They brought instruments used for praise and worship of their God. Even in the midst of their suffering, even in the middle of the frightening and dangerous exodus, even with the Egyptian army on their tails, these women of grace trusted that there would someday be a moment for rejoicing in the Lord.

May we be like those women—always ready to worship and trusting that God will give us a reason to do so. Even when we can't see it just yet on this side of the sea.

---

*Lord, thank You for always giving me ten thousand
reasons to praise Your name. Amen. —M.L.*

Where We Belong

*For just as each of us has one body with many members, and these members
do not all have the same function, so in Christ we, though many, form one body,
and each member belongs to all the others. We have different gifts,
according to the grace given to each of us.*

ROMANS 12:4–6 NIV

*I*magine for a moment what it would be like to go through this life utterly and totally alone. No one to talk to. No one to laugh with. No one to hug or be hugged by. No one to see you. No one to listen. No one to walk with. No one to vent to. No one to lean on.

It's a terrible vision, isn't it?

Thanks be to God who knew we would need each other. He created us to be together. He created us to love and encourage one another. And as a body of believers, we must support one another as we walk together in faith and figure out how to live out the grace of God.

No one needs to be jealous of anyone else, for we are all important. We are all needed. We are all essential. And we are all gifted in different ways.

And this is where we belong. Together. With God. With each other. One body in Christ.

---

*Lord, help me to remember that I belong to You and I belong
to the body of believers. Amen. —M.L.*

Cool It!

Do not be quickly provoked in your spirit,
for anger resides in the lap of fools.
ECCLESIASTES 7:9 NIV

Someone knocks your hot cup of coffee—that third cup that you really, really, really needed right now—out of your hand and it splashes onto your new skirt.

Take a breath. Don't be quickly provoked.

A bad driver pulls out in front of you on a busy road without even looking, making you stomp on your brakes and almost cause a crash.

Easy, now. Keep your hands on the steering wheel. Don't be quickly provoked.

Your coworker "accidentally" took your last piece of homemade pie from the fridge without asking.

Calm down. Don't be quickly provoked.

Your kid took the last bit of toilet paper and didn't replace it and now you are stuck without any. . .again.

Cool it! You'll figure something out. Don't be quickly provoked.

Hooray! Give yourself a pat on the back. You made it through your day without actually yelling at anyone. Now, if we could just work on that "in your spirit" part. . . .

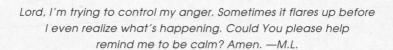

Lord, I'm trying to control my anger. Sometimes it flares up before
I even realize what's happening. Could You please help
remind me to be calm? Amen. —M.L.

Serve One Another

God has given each of you a gift from his great variety of spiritual gifts.
Use them well to serve one another.

1 PETER 4:10 NLT

*S*ometimes people get so caught up in analyzing and assessing and figuring out what spiritual gift they might have, they forget what the gifts are supposed to be for. They are for serving one another and serving God.

If we have a gift of speaking, but we use it to tear down others' arguments or badger someone into bending to our will, we would be wasting our gift. If we have the gift of helping others, but instead only help ourselves, we would be neglecting our responsibility as a member of the family of God.

Instead of worrying overmuch about what gifts we have or don't have, we should focus on what is right in front of us. What need has God brought to our attention today? What help can we offer someone in our community? What has God supplied us with—either in talent or time or treasure that we can use to support someone today. Not for our own glory. Not for thanks. Not for a pat on the back. But simply to serve others and to bring glory to God.

———◆———

Lord, help me to understand what tools I already have
and how I can use them to bring glory to You.
Thank You for every good gift! Amen. —M.L.

One Voice

*May the God who gives endurance and encouragement give you the same
attitude of mind toward each other that Christ Jesus had, so that with
one mind and one voice you may glorify the God and
Father of our Lord Jesus Christ.*

ROMANS 15:5–6 NIV

The chorus of over a hundred singers was amazing to watch. They seemed to even breathe in unison. Every perfectly layered note fell out of their mouths in sweet harmony. Though each section had its own part, and some had solos, the song flowed together—like many threads joining to create a rich and beautiful tapestry.

This is the goal for us as we work and serve together. To be looking out for each other and thinking about the needs of each other to such an extent that we anticipate the issues before they are even spoken. To be appreciating and encouraging one another with the effect of drawing everyone together and uniting us all in the act of serving others. To be in agreement on all the most important aspects of our faith, to listen to the truth, and to hold tightly to the Word of God, so that when we speak about Jesus, no matter what words we use or what accent we have, we may be offering a message of unity.

Many members. One mind. One voice. One beautiful, glorious song of faith.

———◆———

*Lord, I want to glorify You in unity with my brothers and sisters
in Christ. Help me to do that, please. Amen. —M.L.*

Get Wise

Getting wisdom is the wisest thing you can do!
And whatever else you do, develop good judgment.
PROVERBS 4:7 NLT

Should you read all twelve volumes of an encyclopedia series? Should you watch every documentary on human development? Should you go to the library and just live there for a year, soaking it all in?

Though these may all be ways to get some kinds of knowledge, they won't offer the wisdom that the proverb writer is talking about.

We get wisdom when we look to the source of all wisdom. We get wisdom by reading God's Word. We get wisdom by listening to the words of godly men and women. We get wisdom by learning from godly teachers, and then going out and experiencing the world on our own. We get wisdom by taking chances in good faith and making mistakes. We get wisdom by humbly asking for forgiveness along with it.

We get wisdom by spending a long time with the Lord. The more we read His Word and understand His voice, the better we will be able to discern whether things we hear in the world are from Him or not.

We get wisdom by working alongside godly people. The more we watch what they do and how they do it, the better equipped we will be to make our own decisions and take our own steps out into the world.

Lord, make me wise and good and strong,
so I can live for You. Amen. —M.L.

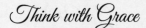

Think with Grace

*Finally, brothers and sisters, whatever is true, whatever is noble,
whatever is right, whatever is pure, whatever is lovely, whatever is admirable—
if anything is excellent or praiseworthy—think about such things.*
PHILIPPIANS 4:8 NIV

*E*very sin we engage in begins as a thought. A little whisper in our minds. A brief glimpse of a tempting vision. An idea. A desire. A bit of deceit. A longing for something that will do us no good at all.

Instead of letting those thoughts multiply and grow into sinful acts and harmful behaviors, fight against them by filling your mind with truth, nobility, righteousness, purity, loveliness, admirable qualities, excellence, and praise.

When the whispering begins, face it with truth from God's Word. When something appeals to your human desires, consider what the most noble and upright person you know might do instead. When your purity is threatened, look to Jesus. Read His words and think about how He lived on this earth—that though He was tempted just like us, He was able to obey God and resist those tempters. When you are met with ugliness, consider all that is beautiful in the world and how God made it just to delight us. When it feels easier to get off the straight and narrow, think about how your actions might lead others into difficulty. When you want to be lazy, consider how excellence glorifies God and acts as a good witness of the life of faith. And when you want to curse, sing songs of praise instead.

Lord, help me to fill my thoughts with Your grace. Amen. —M.L.

Proper Respect

Show proper respect to everyone, love the family of believers,
fear God, honor the emperor.
1 PETER 2:17 NIV

*R*espect takes practice. We are not born as respectful creatures. Respect requires a consideration for the wishes and needs of others.

Babies don't respect anyone. They cry all night and make everyone tired. They ask for unceasing, unlimited attention. They interrupt. . .well, everything. Babies don't think about what others need or want. Babies think about possibly four things: I'm hungry, I'm tired, I want to be held, and I pooped—please fix it.

As we grow into adulthood, parents are the ones who teach us respect. By their actions, they show us how they respect (or don't) others. By their words, they command us to respect them. It's a lesson we get taught over and over and over again. Respect. Rebel. Rebuke. Repeat.

But learning proper respect and how to show it to everyone—from the guy who picks up your trash, to the doctor giving you an exam, to the teacher in your class, to the governor of your area, and so on—gives you the chance to do more than just show consideration for others. You can show love—how you love others and how you love God.

Lord, teach me how to show proper respect to everyone
and correct me when I don't. Amen. —M.L.

Secrets

Inside the Tent of Meeting, the LORD would speak to Moses face to face,
as one speaks to a friend. Afterward Moses would return to the camp,
but the young man who assisted him, Joshua son of Nun,
would remain behind in the Tent of Meeting.

EXODUS 33:11 NLT

Two friends meet for lunch, and just when they begin to share their hearts more deeply, they both pause. They each wonder, *Can I share my secrets without being embarrassed? What will she think of me? Can I truly trust my friend?*

From time to time, all people tend to hide their doubts, their secret thought lives, and their fears.

When you have burdens too heavy to carry, Christ can be trusted. He is listening. He is loving, and He will speak to you as a friend. He is capable of carrying every last pound of your baggage and every one of your burdens. He's powerful enough to bring light to your darkness, calm your feverish doubts, vanquish your foulest fears, and change your world for good.

So, yes, earthly friends can be a blessing, but never hesitate to share your heart with Christ. Never hesitate to embrace the grace!

———◆———

Lord, I am burdened by my fears and my sins and my past.
I choose to trust in You, so I will now share all my life with You,
even the secrets too heavy to carry. Amen. —A.H.

Don't Believe It

And I am convinced that nothing can ever separate us from God's love. Neither death
nor life, neither angels nor demons, neither our fears for today nor our worries about
tomorrow—not even the powers of hell can separate us from God's love. No power
in the sky above or in the earth below—indeed, nothing in all creation will ever be
able to separate us from the love of God that is revealed in Christ Jesus our Lord.

ROMANS 8:38–39 NLT

*Y*ou can hear the dark whispers in your spirit, *Now you've gone and done it.*
You have separated yourself permanently from God with that last transgression.
He'll never take you back now. Or you might hear, *You're a tragic mess, a heap of*
garbage. Too confused, too wishy-washy, too contaminated by the world to be redeemed,
loved, used by God. Two words summarize your life—Give. Up.

Don't you ever believe it! Run away from these spiritual murmurs, since
it is condemnation from the enemy of your soul. Run into the arms of Jesus,
where you will find forgiveness, rest, refreshment, love, and peace. Not to
mention joy! Yes, in the arms of Jesus is just where you belong.

Because nothing will separate you from the love of God. Nothing.

Thank You, Lord, that even when I've been the prodigal daughter,
You will love me and You will welcome me home. Amen. —A.H.

Marvelous Workmanship

You made all the delicate, inner parts of my body and knit me together in
my mother's womb. Thank you for making me so wonderfully complex!
Your workmanship is marvelous—how well I know it.

PSALM 139:13–14 NLT

*W*e spend a lot of time and money trying to stand out in the crowd. We want to brag about unusual adventures we've had that other people have never experienced. We want a unique look that sets us apart from others. We want skills that don't seem run-of-the-mill, but fresh and relevant and useful. We want to stand out in every way!

But no matter how much we try to accomplish that end with human efforts, sometimes we still feel like a snowflake lost in an ordinary bank of snow. But on closer inspection—think macro photography—we discover just the opposite. There is incredible variation in those snowflake crystals. Amazing pristine beauty. Unfathomable design. Spectacular uniqueness to behold.

This is you. This is me. This is all of us.

So, never should you feel like one of the masses. You are not. You are inimitable, created by God for a life of goodness and grace, for brilliance and wonder. And for great purpose!

———◆———

Almighty Creator, I thank You for Your marvelous workmanship.
Thank You that I am wonderfully complex and
beautifully made. Amen. —A.H.

The Pleasure of Your Company

*So the Word became human and made his home among us. He was full of
unfailing love and faithfulness. And we have seen his glory,
the glory of the Father's one and only Son.*

JOHN 1:14 NLT

*J*esus was born on earth not only because He wanted to save us from
our transgressions, but to make a home with us and to get to know us.
He wanted the pleasure of our company, and He still does. Imagine!

According to God's Word, He even keeps track of the hairs on our heads.
Now, that's loving all the details of our lives! Yes, God wants to know your
favorite flower, your favorite Christmas foods, and your favorite funny words
that make you grin—like *fusspot*, *higgledy-piggledy*, or *kerfuffle*. He wants to
know what makes you sad or glad, and what makes you laugh so hard you
can barely breathe.

Remember His longing for Your company as you think of all the many
busy things you want to pack into your day. Do you choose to spend time
with Him that you might enjoy each other's company?

*Oh Lord, You are my best and dearest friend. Show me how to be as
faithful and loving to You as You have been to me. Amen. —A.H.*

The Gardenias by Your Door

There was a believer in Joppa named Tabitha (which in Greek is Dorcas).
She was always doing kind things for others and helping the poor.
ACTS 9:36 NLT

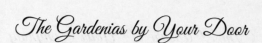

The little girl was insistent that she wanted to give the older neighbor lady a surprise—a tiny bouquet of gardenias from their garden. The mother had taught her daughter well, that deeds of kindness were worth more than all the fine toys in the world. And she believed it. So, the girl gingerly set the jar of white flowers by the front door, rang the bell, and then ran with her mom toward home. But even though the older woman would never know who gave her the fragrant gift, she called out, "Thank you, whoever you are!"

And that little girl never forgot the hope and joy she put in the older woman's voice that day. She never forgot the delight of giving. She grew up not only following Christ but loving the verses in the Bible about Tabitha, a woman of many kind deeds. And the little girl—who became a grown woman of grace and good deeds—brought smiles of hope and joy to many a heart, including the heart of God.

———◆———

Lord, I love the story of Tabitha in the Bible, and I love her generous
spirit. Please help me to be a woman of many kind deeds,
especially to the poor. Amen. —A.H.

In the Light of Eternity

If we could put the whole of the universe inside a box, then what is outside that box? More of the same—more of the universe? And if we could put time in a box, then what is outside that box of time? More time? In our finite thinking, these infinite concepts are impossible to grasp. Our existence and even our imaginations are bound by the physical limits of this earth.

But what we can know and appreciate is that our earthly journey is but a short one. At times, our pain and suffering and troubles feel never-ending, but when one thinks in terms of eternal life through Christ, the moments of travail will pass in less than a heartbeat.

In moments when you have need—when the world's pain seems too great and you long for heaven—remember your days in the light of eternity. The Lord will never leave you now, and in His perfect timing—He will call you home to a new and beautiful life that knows no end.

Lord, thank You for the timeless hope of heaven! Amen. —A.H.

Flying Free

*All of us have become like one who is unclean, and all our righteous
acts are like filthy rags; we all shrivel up like a leaf,
and like the wind our sins sweep us away.*

ISAIAH 64:6 NIV

*I*n a magnificent garden handmade by God, mankind was meant to delight in life—to fly free of sin and walk with their Creator. But amazingly, humans wanted more than paradise with the Almighty. In a deliberate act of rebellion—believing they could become gods—the first two humans fell from grace. One could say that their wings were singed by pride. And now all of us—even our most beautiful deeds—are tinged with that same stain of the soul.

Not I, you might say!

But do you sing in the church choir to use your gifts for God, glorifying Him, or is your performance laced with self-importance? Did you fast that meal in private, or did you drop a few hints about your sacrifice so people would think well of you? Did you mean the compliment you gave your boss, or was it flattery to get that raise?

The finest of intentions and the best love offerings to God can be easily spoiled. Bits of pride cling to our spirits. Oh, how they resist being shaken off. But with the Lord's help, we can prevail!

———◆———

*Holy Spirit, please root out in me all that is tinged with sin.
I want to be the beautiful creature You made me to be. Amen. —A.H.*

Friends for All Time

Come close to God, and God will come close to you. Wash your hands, you sinners;
purify your hearts, for your loyalty is divided between God and the world.
JAMES 4:8 NLT

*Y*ou found this friend, and boy, is she a keeper. You understand each other. You share your secrets and your heart—all of it—the tears and trials, the joys and triumphs. You truly enjoy spending time with each other. You don't even have to talk all the time, since you both seem to know each other so well that you are content to just be in each other's company. And so, you two become inseparable—friends for life. Ahh, what a blessing.

How can that relate to the Lord? As followers of Christ, we should feel so close to Him that we become inseparable friends—through this life and in the life to come. We will share our secrets and our hearts. We will commune with Him, grow in understanding and grace, and we will enjoy basking in the light and love of His presence.

Who can resist such divine friendship, such eternal love?

Yes, oh yes, may we all come close to God!

———◆———

Lord, I haven't been following You as I should. My loyalties have indeed
been divided. Wash away my sins and purify my heart. I want us
to be close always. In Jesus' name I pray, amen. —A.H.

Those Reflective Moments

Jesus looked at them and said, "With man this is impossible,
but with God all things are possible."
MATTHEW 19:26 NIV

*D*o you ever have one of those reflective moments when you look into the mirror and say, "I am meant for more than this"?

Everyone has experienced those spiritual nudges from the Holy Spirit—when they feel there is way more out there than what they are currently experiencing.

Maybe you feel the rough and dirty edges of some life-rut—a pothole you can't pull out of with your own willpower and grit. Was there more you had wanted to accomplish in your lifetime? Dreams that continue to go un-realized? Are you using your God-given talents and gifts? Are there pet sins you still cling to—bits of pride, disobedience, or unforgiveness—that are holding you back from meeting your full potential in Christ?

Use those reflective life-moments. Prayerfully make a list of all the things you feel God wants you to do, to be. Even if it seems impossible. With man it *will be* impossible. But with God, ah yes—all things become possible.

Oh Lord, I feel I've been in a rut, and I want out. But I know I can only
do it with Your guidance, Your courage, and Your supernatural
power. I want to be all that You created me to be!
Thank You for Your grace and mercy. Amen. —A.H.

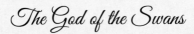

The God of the Swans

*One thing I have asked of the LORD, and that I will seek: That I may dwell
in the house of the LORD [in His presence] all the days of my life, to gaze upon
the beauty [the delightful loveliness and majestic grandeur]
of the LORD, and to meditate in His temple.*

PSALM 27:4 AMP

Think of the most beautiful things in the world. Iridescent butterflies?
A thunderhead lit by a sunset? The glide of a black swan on a silvery
lake? God is not only the master Creator of all things beautiful, but God is
beautiful too!

People in turn long to make things of beauty from all the gifts He has
given us on earth. And the fulfillment of this exquisite spiritual ache connects
us to Him in a way that is both mystical and very real.

We are made in God's image. Imagine. We belong to Him, and we also
long to be with Him, even when we don't admit it. That darkened void in
our lives can only be filled with His holy breath. Our fallen souls can only be
healed by His grace. And we can only be brought to a place of beauty within
our souls by His holy presence. How divine and mysterious are these thoughts!
But oh, how beautiful is our God!

---◆---

*Lord, may I dwell in Your presence all the days of my life.
May I gaze upon Your delightful loveliness and
majestic grandeur forever. Amen. —A.H.*

Hang On!

Wait on the LORD; be of good courage,
and He shall strengthen your heart; wait, I say, on the LORD!
PSALM 27:14 NKJV

There is that one leaf left on the tree. It has gone brown and crispy and lifeless—trembling on the branch—and yet for some reason, it hangs on. The evening shadows grow drearier, the air colder, and the wind whips the poor thing to the point that it looks like it will surely let go.

Does that image reflect a season in your life? Dried up? Dull and lifeless? You sense too keenly that sharp wind of adversity, trying to tear you off the tree of life? Maybe you want to let go of that branch, never to be seen again?

You are not alone in your troubles. Don't give up. Not on life. Not on hope. Not on God.

Hang on. Wait on the Lord. He will see you through. Cling to the Lord's promises. Only God has the love and the grace and the power to sustain you!

Oh Lord, please comfort me in these trials. Help me to hang on in the midst of loneliness and grief and sufferings. I will wait on You, believing You will strengthen my heart. In Jesus' name I pray, amen. —A.H.

Baggage Hitting Baggage

"He himself bore our sins" in his body on the cross, so that we might die
to sins and live for righteousness; "by his wounds you have been healed."

1 PETER 2:24 NIV

*I*f you put two people in a room with painful emotional baggage—that is, issues that have never been dealt with—be sure and step out of the way. There's going to be trouble.

Woman number one might say something with no initial intended guile, but the other woman—because of her wounded history—may comprehend the words as offensive. After a bristling retort from woman number two, the first woman's courteous veneer may melt away like rice paper in a fire. Then that's it. No more propped-up kindness. No more pasted-on smiles. Whammo! It's baggage hitting baggage. And it's not a pretty sight.

So what do we do with all that history and all that pain-filled past? We give it to God. Sound too easy? Too trite?

And yet the Word reminds us that "by his wounds we have been healed." In every way. Body, spirit, emotions. All of it. The Lord wants us to be able to move forward into the future, because constantly looking back will only cause us to stumble in the present and fear for the future. May we always choose grace—His grace.

Holy Spirit, free me from my past, all of it.
I trust in You fully to set me free! Amen. —A.H.

Diversions

I am saying this for your benefit, not to place restrictions on you.
I want you to do whatever will help you serve the Lord best,
with as few distractions as possible.
1 CORINTHIANS 7:35 NLT

This world is loaded with stuff to do. Meetings to schedule. Parties to attend. Games to play. Goodies to buy. Movies to watch. Hobbies to take up. Delicacies to be relished. Destinations to travel to. Photos to post. Pianos to be practiced. Dreams to be chased. Exercises to be carried out. Meals to prepare. Careers to be pursued. Pets to care for. Friends to hang out with. Fun to be had.

You get the idea. All good things, but if we take on too much, we can forget God is even there. That He is the giver of all gifts and deserves our time. Our listening heart. Our love. Our worship.

So when the gifts of life become no more than mere distractions, it's time to reassess. Maybe we could ask ourselves these questions: "Am I considering the Lord's will for my life? Do I spend quiet time with the Lord? Am I 'doing life *with* God' or 'am I distracted *from* God?' " And "Am I so driven inside the temporal world that I have forgotten what is eternal?"

Lord, help me to love You so much that staying focused on
You becomes the best part of my life! Amen. —A.H.

Withhold No Good Thing

For the LORD God is our sun and our shield. He gives us grace and glory.
The LORD will withhold no good thing from those who do what is right.
PSALM 84:11 NLT

*Y*ou tried and tried until you finally learned how to make that chicken cordon bleu. You tasted it, and ahh, what a blue-ribbon success it was! So you placed it on the table with high hopes. Yes, the family came. They ate. They wiped their mouths. Then they scooted their chairs back and left.

And your heart wilted like a flower left on a hot windowsill.

The darker side of you lamented, "Pearls before swine! Never again!" But, of course, you didn't mean it. Well, maybe a little. Seriously, you would do it again and again for them, because you love them dearly. But couldn't someone have been thankful? Couldn't they have raved over the work and the love just a little? Yes, they could have. Perhaps you should share your feelings on the matter. But what a sadness that we travel through this life running on so little support, so little kindness and encouragement.

God withholds no good thing from us when we do what is right. Shouldn't we do the same for others?

Lord, may I always offer encouraging words
to those who need it. Amen. —A.H.

Two Beautiful Words

"Who can hide in secret places so that I cannot see them?" declares the Lord.
"Do not I fill heaven and earth?" declares the Lord.

JEREMIAH 23:24 NIV

*Y*our little boy is as cute as a bug's ear as he moves stealthily under the sheet, thinking you cannot see his form bobbing around. Or your little dumpling girl closes her eyes, believing you cannot see her if she cannot see you. But alas, you're an all-seeing mom in this case, and you think their antics are adorable.

Even as adults, we have all done our share of hiding, especially from God. But the whys and ways aren't so adorable. This has been the modus operandi of mankind since the beginning, as we can see in Genesis 3:8 (NIV): "Then the man and his wife heard the sound of the Lord God as he was walking in the garden in the cool of the day, and they hid from the Lord God among the trees of the garden."

After the fall in Eden or even today at this very moment—how easy it is to forget that God sees all we do. We cannot hide. Nor should we. May we always step out into the light of Christ and embrace two beautiful and life-changing words—*grace* and *repentance*.

———◆———

Lord, I admit I have been trying to hide some of my sins from You, and I know that is such spiritual foolishness. Please forgive me, and set me on the path of righteousness! Amen. —A.H.

Our Bottle of Energy

"Therefore I tell you, do not worry about your life, what you will eat or drink;
or about your body, what you will wear. Is not life more than food, and the body
more than clothes? Look at the birds of the air; they do not sow or reap or store away
in barns, and yet your heavenly Father feeds them. Are you not much more valuable
than they? Can any one of you by worrying add a single hour to your life?"
MATTHEW 6:25–27 NIV

*M*any people feel they don't have enough energy to make it through the week. They run out of steam too soon. But energy can be spent in many ways. We each get a daily allotment, depending on our age, health, and other factors. And we each have to decide how to use our bottle of energy, no matter how large or how small. We can use precious drops on various emotions such as anger, grumbling, and the big one—worry—or we can treasure that bottle of energy and divvy it out for more important things like creating, praising, working, encouraging, laughing, serving, loving, and rejoicing!

It's our choice. Every. Single. Day.

How do you choose to use your bottle of energy today?

———◆———

Oh Lord, I admit I worry too much, and by the end of the day I'm
exhausted from it. Help me to trust in You fully and to use my
energy for what You want me to do. Amen. —A.H.

By Invitation Only

For the grace of God has appeared that
offers salvation to all people.
Titus 2:11 NIV

*Y*ou suddenly see a door at the back of the room you've never seen before. You see a small plaque that's etched in gold, which reads, BY INVITATION ONLY. Suddenly, someone breezes by you and through the sliding door, without even a glance at you. Obviously, they belong in there. And well, you don't.

A range of emotions surge through you. Sadness at being left out. Stubbornness making you want to storm through the door to beg for an invitation. And then you might feel envy as you give up and walk back to your corner of the room. We have all felt these pangs from being the uninvited ones. But thank God that the most important invitation of a lifetime is for every person. Everyone!

Second Peter 3:9 (NIV) reminds us, "The Lord is not slow in keeping his promise, as some understand slowness. Instead he is patient with you, not wanting anyone to perish, but everyone to come to repentance."

God is clear when He says, "All people are invited to heaven." He wants no one to perish. But we do have to receive His offer—the gift of salvation through Christ.

Have you accepted this grace-filled invitation?

———◆———

Lord, I thank You for Your gift of salvation. I repent of my sins.
I accept You as my Lord and Savior. And I look forward
to spending eternity with You. Amen. —A.H.

Hotline

Give all your worries and cares to God, for he cares about you. Stay alert!
Watch out for your great enemy, the devil. He prowls around
like a roaring lion, looking for someone to devour.

1 PETER 5:7–8 NLT

Sometimes when life goes wrong—very wrong—you feel stripped of pretense and masks. You feel emotionally bare before God and men. You might even fear you are all alone. Your thoughts become gritty with terrors. Your replies might be sharp. You are shaken to the core of your soul, and you almost forget how to pray. You need God.

Now.

God's hotline may seem nebulous, but it is genuine. Turn to Him. He is there. He is listening. And He not only cares for you but has the mighty power to help you through whatever it is that is plaguing you. Whatever it is that is holding you back. Whatever it is that the enemy of your soul is trying to destroy. Take heart—God is still in control of all things, including your life. His mercy is real and His love endures forever!

———◆———

Lord, I can't do life alone. I have tried until I'm bone weary and filled
with anxiety. I desperately need Your supernatural help in every
way. Please be with me now and help me in my
dark hour of trouble. Amen. —A.H.

What's Real

The heavens proclaim the glory of God. The skies display his craftsmanship.
Day after day they continue to speak; night after night they make him known.
They speak without a sound or word; their voice is never heard. Yet their
message has gone throughout the earth, and their words to all
the world. God has made a home in the heavens for the sun.

PSALM 19:1–4 NLT

$\mathcal{I}$t's one of your all-time favorite movies, and you can't get over how real that Hollywood set looks. So many details. Spaceship dials that surely must blast the craft into orbit. Distant mountains and verdant valleys. And western streets bustling with spirited women and noble cowboys.

But if you take a tour of the movie sets, you'll find that some of what you thought was real is no more than props, painted backdrops, and facades. Understandable but a little disheartening.

On the other hand, when you look behind God's handiwork and His promises, it's all real. No pretending here. The heavens shout the glory of God. The skies display His handiwork. If we listen, we can hear the message of His majesty, His beauty, and His truth.

Know and take comfort in this—when the world builds you a paper moon, you can celebrate what has always been real. God's world is authentic, His promises can be counted on, and His grace is more than sufficient!

---◆---

Lord, I trust You that You are all the light and love
and truth this world needs! Amen. —A.H.

Embrace the Grace

Whoever believes in the Son has eternal life, but whoever rejects the Son will not see life, for God's wrath remains on them.
JOHN 3:36 NIV

When a child grows up in the church, it's easy for her to ride on the spiritual coattails of her parents. She may be encouraged to do all the right stuff—attend church, listen to family Bible readings, pray before bed. You consider yourselves to be a good Christian family. But when it comes to your daughter's own decision, has she embraced the grace—has her knowledge of Christ moved from her head down to her heart?

Without that personal decision for Christ, what will happen when that child starts a life journey of her own? She could find herself questioning the beliefs of her family, doubting the need for church attendance, drifting toward cults and false religions, or doubting the existence of God all together. When we go out in the world powered only by the fumes of our family's faith, we're inevitably going to run out of steam and experience a crisis of belief. According to scripture, making one's own decision for Christ is the only way to freedom, forgiveness, and eternal life.

So has your knowledge of Christ moved from your head down to your heart? Have you embraced the grace?

I choose You, Jesus, as my Lord and Savior. Please forgive me for my sins and be ever near me. I look forward to an eternity with You! Amen. —A.H.

Unleash the Joy!

Simon Peter, when he saw it, fell to his knees before Jesus. "Master, leave. I'm a sinner and can't handle this holiness. Leave me to myself." When they pulled in that catch of fish, awe overwhelmed Simon and everyone with him. It was the same with James and John, Zebedee's sons, coworkers with Simon.

LUKE 5:8–10 MSG

Maybe you've thought, *I've done it now. . . . I have committed this sin one too many times. God couldn't possibly forgive me now.* Or, *This sin is too terrible for the Lord to deal with.* Like Simon Peter, you want to tell the Lord to go away from you because you can't handle His holiness.

Don't let the sly whispers of Satan fool you into thinking you're a lost cause. You're not. God has the last say. Christ's redemptive power is available to you, no matter what. When every natural inclination is to run away in shame for what you've done, do the opposite—run into the merciful and grace-filled arms of Jesus. Your repentant heart may find a loving reproof, but it will also find forgiveness. It will also discover rest. And your heart will unleash such joy!

His grace is ours for the taking. Accept it. Love it. Thank God for it.

———◆———

Lord, I thank You and praise You for Your compassion and Your forgiveness. Amen. —A.H.

The Little Things Mean a Lot

In the city of Joppa there was a woman named Dorcas ("Gazelle"),
a believer who was always doing kind things for others, especially for the poor.
ACTS 9:36 TLB

The homeless woman looked mighty cold in the winter wind, so you not only took off your coat and placed it around her shoulders, but you bought her a hot meal. You weeded the flower bed of the new mom who needed a helping hand. The elderly widower next door looked lonely, so you sat with him awhile and listened to his stories.

When you have time, read the whole heartwarming story of Dorcas in Acts 9:36–43: about how her good deeds helped many people, about how she miraculously rose from the dead after Peter prayed over her, and how the news of that supernatural event caused many people to believe in the Lord.

Sometimes the little things do mean a lot. The ripple effect can be never-ending. And sometimes they have the power to change a life. What acts of kindness can you do today that might make God smile? That might change a life forever?

Lord, give me a heart for the poor and needy. Teach me how to have
a spirit of compassion, kindness, and generosity, and may I do
it all for Your glory. In Jesus' name I pray, amen. —A.H.

The Iron Tree

Finally, my brethren, be strong in the Lord and in the power of His might.
Put on the whole armor of God, that you may be able
to stand against the wiles of the devil.
EPHESIANS 6:10–11 NKJV

In God's creation, the New Zealand Christmas tree or iron tree is a remarkable thing to see. It's dazzling in color, strong in stature, beautiful to behold, and it can grow on stony cliffs—precarious places that seem unlikely to support life. And yet the iron tree not only survives there—it thrives.

What a great image as we ponder the Christian life. How are we holding up in this dark world and how do we respond when we're hit with the fiery darts of the devil? As Christians, may we always be more like the iron tree. May we grow sturdier every day. Strong in the Lord and in the power of His might. May we dazzle all those around us with the light of Christ, and may our love be beautiful to behold!

Holy Spirit, please guide me in Your ways. Make me strong and beautiful and full of Your holy light that I might not only stand strong against the enemy but that I might be a witness of Your saving grace. Amen. —A.H.

The Rain of Heaven
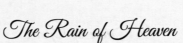

"His master replied, 'Well done, good and faithful servant! You have been faithful with a few things; I will put you in charge of many things. Come and share your master's happiness!' "

MATTHEW 25:23 NIV

We can sense it when we've done well for God. We can feel it deep in our souls. We may have fulfilled a task that we knew the Lord asked us to do. Maybe we encouraged someone who had become brokenhearted. Or we earned enough from our wise investments to help people in distress. Or we told others about the Lord's gift of grace when they were lost.

From the world's vantage point, faithfulness to the Lord sounds like an archaic way to live—perhaps too cringingly self-sacrificing for our tastes. Not enough "me" in that equation. But God's way is the only road to true happiness. To bring God joy spills over onto us. One might call it the glorious rain of heaven. And when we are faithful, He promises to trust us with even more. How marvelous.

Oh to hear those words: "Well done, good and faithful servant! You have been faithful with a few things; I will put you in charge of many things. Come and share your master's happiness!"

———◆———

Lord, may I be trustworthy in all I do! Amen. —A.H.

A Sign of Grace

"And I seal this promise with this sign: I have placed my rainbow in the clouds
as a sign of my promise until the end of time, to you and to all the earth.
When I send clouds over the earth, the rainbow will be seen in the clouds,
and I will remember my promise to you and to every being,
that never again will the floods come and destroy all life."

GENESIS 9:12–15 TLB

It is said that a rainbow is the refraction, reflection, and dispersion of light through water droplets, which causes it to break down into its constituent colors. Remember Roy G. Biv in school?

But God says there is much more to know about the rainbow's origins beyond what we can learn scientifically. The rainbow is a sign to all mankind. Yes, that glorious painted arc in the clouds is an emblem of mercy—a promise from God Almighty that He will never again destroy the earth and its inhabitants with a flood.

Even in mankind's continued rebellion against all that is good and lovely and holy, the Lord still loves His beloved creation and His promises continue to show us those tender mercies.

———————◆———————

Thank You, God, for Your many promises, for they are a perfect
balance of justice and mercy. In Jesus' name I pray, amen. —A.H.

Bringing God to the People

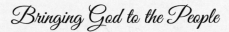

So we are ambassadors for Christ, as though God were making His appeal through us; we [as Christ's representatives] plead with you on behalf of Christ to be reconciled to God.

2 CORINTHIANS 5:20 AMP

Once you accept Christ as your Savior, you then become a representative of Christ and His message of salvation.

"What? Me? Represent Christ? That sounds pretty heavy. Too much spiritual responsibility. If you don't mind, I'd rather go home and watch my favorite TV show now. I will choose to live a more private Christian life and leave the witnessing to the expert theologians and ministers out there."

But Christians are not called to be silent about their faith. Yes, witnessing is an awesome task, and it might seem a bit daunting, and yet as Christians we have the power of the Holy Spirit to help us with this holy quest for souls.

We should think of our mission in terms of telling how Christ's love has changed us. His extravagant, priceless, contagious kind of love. His redemptive, beautiful, powerful kind of love that changes all of life now and for all eternity.

So who can you love into the kingdom today?

---◆---

Holy Spirit, please tell me whom You'd like me to witness to today. I am happy to be an instrument of Your love by telling others of Your sweet Gospel message. Amen. —A.H.

Ask God

"I no longer call you servants, because a servant does not know his master's business. Instead, I have called you friends, for everything that I learned from my Father I have made known to you."

JOHN 15:15 NIV

"Mom, why do the butterflies start out as wiggly worms? Why do I see alligators in the clouds? Why did God make four seasons and not just one big long summer? Why can't I turn off gravity and float like a balloon? Why don't birds roar and lions sing?" Fun kid questions, eh?

Have you ever had questions of your own for God? He may not give you all the answers you want, but since the Lord calls you His friend, He will tell you not only things you need to hear, but perhaps things of wonder. Listen to the Lord. Walk with Him closely. He will surprise you. For our God made you to be curious and creative and full of wonder. So go ahead and ask God. He'd love to hear from you!

———◆———

*Mighty God, I have a zillion questions about this life and this earth and the life to come. Shall we visit awhile? I love You, and I want to get to know You and Your world better every day.
In Jesus' name I pray, amen. —A.H.*

192

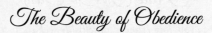

The Beauty of Obedience

*All these blessings will come on you and accompany you if you obey the LORD
your God: You will be blessed in the city and blessed in the country. The fruit of
your womb will be blessed, and the crops of your land and the young of your
livestock—the calves of your herds and the lambs of your flocks. Your basket
and your kneading trough will be blessed. You will be blessed
when you come in and blessed when you go out.*

DEUTERONOMY 28:2–6 NIV

*O*bey. The word tends to make our smiles fade and our spirits wince.
Even as kids, obeying our parents was not at the top of our fun list.
Not even close.

But God says that if you obey Him you are promised blessings. Some
would say that translates into your stocks going through the roof, which might
mean enjoying a much needed addition to your home or the pleasure of a
long-awaited vacation. But it also might mean deep-down joy. It might mean
the blessing of a child. It might mean plenty for your family to eat. It might
mean love for all mankind, even when love is hard to come by. It might mean
biblical understanding and walking nearer to God.

Blessings come in many forms, but anything from God is good.

———◆———

*Lord, I want to obey You in all things, not just to receive Your blessings,
but I want to obey You because I love You dearly. Amen. —A.H.*

Hate Is So Easy

"But I say to you, love [that is, unselfishly seek the best or higher good for] your enemies and pray for those who persecute you."
MATTHEW 5:44 AMP

*Y*ou're going to be on the plane for thirteen hours, and the couple next to you has a screaming baby. Oy! You have tried earplugs. You've tried to sleep, to listen to music, to watch a movie, and to knock yourself out with melatonin, but you can't escape the screeching. You are exhausted from too much racket and nobody seems to care, least of all the parents who seem blissfully ignorant of the misery they have caused.

You're tempted to give them a piece of your mind. But you hold back, trying to keep your anger in check like a good Christian, only to find yourself moments later loathing their very existence.

What can you do? Perhaps ask if they need assistance? If that doesn't seem appropriate, you can pray for the baby, the couple, yourself, the flight attendants, and all the other people affected by the sound. Prayer will not only help that poor couple who must also be exhausted, but the prayers will change you as well.

Next time, though, maybe you should invest in some noise-canceling headphones!

---◆---

Lord, forgive me that when hate comes calling sometimes I've opened the door to it. I know that is not the way for a Christ follower to act. Teach me Your ways of love and forgiveness. Amen. —A.H.

If You Had a Life Song

But seek first his kingdom and his righteousness,
and all these things will be given to you as well.

MATTHEW 6:33 NIV

If someone could write a song about your life, what do you think the lyrics might be like?

Would the song have a quality that reflects "Doing life my way"? Or would it have an "It's all about me" tone? Or would the words have a more heavenly slant, full of truth and grace? Would it be a love song to God and to all of humanity? Would the lyrics reveal what or who is at the center of your life?

Probing thoughts. So what *do* you place there in that beloved heart-hub of your life? Luke 12:34 (NIV) reads, "For where your treasure is, there your heart will be also." How true is that? Because the one thing we spend most of our time and energy and money on is usually the thing that we place in that central, hallowed spot in our lives.

Think about it. Where is your treasure? Who do you love best? The Lord Jesus? Wonderful. Is He showcased in your life song?

———◆———

Lord, I want to put You in the center of my life. Show me
how to do that, not just in a general way, but in a
powerful, daily kind of way! Amen. —A.H.

The Role of the Fool

*He who trusts confidently in his own heart is a [dull, thickheaded] fool,
but he who walks in [skillful and godly] wisdom will be rescued.*
PROVERBS 28:26 AMP

The enemy of our souls loves to play on our impulses. He craves the evil, mischief, trouble, and injury that can come from living a life led by selfish whims and fleshly urges—that is, prideful decisions that do not line up with the precepts of the Bible. The book of Proverbs has a few uncomfortable warnings about such a mind-set. It reminds us that to feel confident in one's own heart is to be a dull and thickheaded fool.

Oh dear!

No one truly wants to line up to play the fool on earth's stage. So, what now? God tells us to humble ourselves. To seek out wise counsel and follow it. To study and learn from His holy Word. There is no need for waywardness. We can be rescued. We can live free.

May we all choose to live a life full of humility and wisdom and grace!

Holy Spirit, guide me in all things. Help me not to be overly confident in myself. Show me how I can keep from being swept away on the waves of impulsive living. Humble me that I might seek godly counsel and walk in wisdom. Amen. —A.H.

To Kiss the Face of God

Then he turned to the woman and said to Simon, "Look! See this woman kneeling here! When I entered your home, you didn't bother to offer me water to wash the dust from my feet, but she has washed them with her tears and wiped them with her hair. You refused me the customary kiss of greeting, but she has kissed my feet again and again from the time I first came in. You neglected the usual courtesy of olive oil to anoint my head, but she has covered my feet with rare perfume."

LUKE 7:44–46 TLB

Can you imagine giving up the chance to kiss the face of God?

Many times when we read these verses in Luke 7, we miss this one part about the customary greeting. Look closely. Simon not only offended the Lord with his judgmental attitude, but he forfeited the chance to kiss Him. Why? Did Simon not believe Jesus was the Son of God? It appears so from reading the whole passage. Simon lacked commitment and faith, but the prostitute believed Jesus fully, repented utterly, and loved Jesus with her heart and soul.

If given the chance, would we hold back, or would we choose to kiss the face of God?

———◆———

Lord Jesus, on the day of my arrival in heaven, I hope to run into Your arms and to kiss Your holy cheek. I love You and adore You! Amen. —A.H.

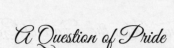

A Question of Pride

The whole Bible was given to us by inspiration from God and is useful to teach us what is true and to make us realize what is wrong in our lives; it straightens us out and helps us do what is right.

2 TIMOTHY 3:16 TLB

"I am right. I'm always right, so please don't bother trying to correct me!" Yes, our spirits romance such prideful thoughts every day, whether we admit it or not. We are fallen creatures, but we still live under a grand illusion. People not only don't want to be corrected, but they don't like being told they have sinned and that they need repentance. And yet the Bible tells us of God's corrections and rebukes, as well as of His love and grace.

Modern man has drifted so far from God and His holiness that some people feel a need to rewrite the Bible. But if we take out all the parts of the Bible that offend us, it will no longer be the Word of God. It will be the book of man.

We have become a pride-filled nation and world, and pride is the very emotion that caused mankind to fall in the first place.

———————◆———————

*Lord, forgive me for trying to run the world on my own.
I am in need of You and Your holy Word. May I never
try to change a word of the Bible! Amen. —A.H.*

Steps to Mercy

"I tell you, love your enemies. Help and give without expecting a return. You'll never—I promise—regret it. Live out this God-created identity the way our Father lives toward us, generously and graciously, even when we're at our worst. Our Father is kind; you be kind."

LUKE 6:36 MSG

When we mean someone harm, even if only to divvy out a disparaging word, it is hard to look them straight in the eye, isn't it? It's easier to do the damage within the safe confines of a crowd or from a distance. Or on social media where we can't see the tears that might trickle down the cheeks of those we've pierced with our careless words.

But seeing people, really seeing them through the eyes of God's balance of justice and mercy, well, it's a real game changer. No longer can we make sweeping judgments and harsh criticisms when we see the face of the person whom we have sentenced with our decrees or words. Because seeing is one step away from understanding, and understanding is one step closer to mercy.

◆

Lord, help me to see people with Your holy eyes of compassion, and help me remember all the many times You were kind to me even when I was at my worst. In Jesus' name I pray, amen. —A.H.

Oh, How I Cherish You!

A third time he asked him, "Simon son of John, do you love me?" Peter was hurt that Jesus asked the question a third time. He said, "Lord, you know everything. You know that I love you." Jesus said, "Then feed my sheep."
JOHN 21:17 NLT

As you rock that baby ever-so-gently in your arms—back and forth, back and forth—you hum lullabies and whisper sweet nothings into her ears. You sprinkle kisses on her head and her eyelids flutter shut as she falls into dreaming. Oh, how your heart aches with love for your wee one. You'd do anything for her!

How do we love the Lord? Jesus not only asked Peter about his love but He asks us too: "Do you love me?" Does your heart ache with love for your Lord? Do you cherish Him? Would you do anything for Him? Have you said those beloved words to Him today? "Jesus, I love You most dearly!" Love is an emotion, but it can also be displayed in actions. Do you care for the Lord enough to let your words be transformed into love deeds for others? This is another way to love God—by loving others.

Lord, I'm sorry I haven't told You lately how much I love You and cherish You. You are my everything, and I want to feed Your sheep with the good news of Your Gospel! Amen. —A.H.

Approaching God?

"In the morning you will see the glory of the LORD, because he has heard your complaints, which are against him, not against us. What have we done that you should complain about us?" Then Moses added, "The LORD will give you meat to eat in the evening and bread to satisfy you in the morning, for he has heard all your complaints against him. What have we done? Yes, your complaints are against the LORD, not against us."

EXODUS 16:7–8 NLT

When someone at work is known for constant complaining, what do you do when you see them coming down the hallway? If you're smart, you'll look busy on your phone and speed walk the other way!

How do we approach God when we have our devotion time—with gratitude or grousing? Instead of begging and whining and saying, "Why can't You do something about my many prayers?" might it be better and more loving to come before the Lord with praise first? Our Lord can handle our heavy laments, it's true. We know this from the many heart cries in the Psalms. And yet the Lord wants us to come before Him with praise and song too, so that we might meet the day with expectation and joy and thankfulness!

Lord, show me how to please You in all I do, even in the way I come before You each day in prayer. Amen. —A.H.

The Perfect Day

"In My Father's house are many mansions; if it were not so, I would have told you.
I go to prepare a place for you. And if I go and prepare a place for you, I will come
again and receive you to Myself; that where I am, there you may be also.
And where I go you know, and the way you know."

JOHN 14:2–4 NKJV

*H*ave you ever had a perfect day? The sun is warm; the breeze is silky cool. The perfume of some heavenly blossom fills the air along with the sweet sounds of laughter. You relax and breathe deeply. You are with your favorite people and, wow, life is good. Even the finest day of our lives, though, will not even come close to one sublime day in eternity with God.

The Lord has made a promise to us. Jesus said He has gone to prepare a place for us. There are mansions in this kingdom called heaven, and you can be sure they are far beyond any gilded glory we've seen on earth. He also promised to come again and receive those who love Him and obey Him. Of all the homecomings we've known on earth, this will be the grandest and the most joy infused. This is a homecoming not to be missed!

Thank You, heavenly Father, that because of Your gift of salvation
through Christ, I have the hope of heaven! Amen. —A.H.

The Enduring Attribute of Love

The one who does not love has not become acquainted with God
[does not and never did know Him], for God is love. [He is the originator
of love, and it is an enduring attribute of His nature.]

1 John 4:8 AMP

*H*ave you embraced God's love? It is beautiful. Sacrificial. Lavish. Irresistible.

And yet we do have free will. You can choose to reject God's love. You can flee. You can live outside His beloved circle.

But why would a person make such a choice? Could it be that pride has gotten in the way of good sense? That we have sacrificed pure, sweet love for a counterfeit version that will only bring destruction and despair?

In 1 John 4:16 (AMP), we read, "We have come to know [by personal observation and experience], and have believed [with deep, consistent faith] the love which God has for us. God is love, and the one who abides in love abides in God, and God abides *continually* in him."

Oh to love with a whole heart and be drenched in the light and love of Christ. And to have the Lord abide with us continually! That is the way of heaven. That is God's way.

———◆———

Thank You, Lord, for Your exquisite and sacrificial
and lavish love for me. I love You too! Amen. —A.H.

What Was Once Broken

He heals the brokenhearted and binds up their wounds
[healing their pain and comforting their sorrow].
Psalm 147:3 AMP

You've had a splendiferous afternoon beachcombing, and you've found the most beautiful shells you've ever seen. You take your treasure trove home and weed out the ones that are cracked or faded, or that are missing a piece. You place only the perfect, prettiest ones in a little collection on the coffee table as a tribute to that wonderful day on the beach.

The rest get tossed. Why? Somewhere deep down we don't like looking at the shells that are broken. Maybe it's too sharp a reminder of our own world—our own lives.

Chips of sin here and there. Bits of sandy dirt that has never been washed away. And an overall lack of luster from being battered in the ocean and baked on the hot sands.

We don't like to display our brokenness. We want to hide it, toss it, pretend it was never there.

But we need to hold up our failings to God. He has more than enough love for us to wash us clean, to heal the broken places, and to give us that brilliant luster back.

The Lord wants us so beautiful that the world will stop and ponder. They will gather us in so they too might find the way—His way—to become the treasures we were meant to be!

———◆———

Thank You, Lord, for making me whole and beautiful. Amen. —A.H.

The Sweet Fragrance of Mercy!

See to it that no one falls short of God's grace; that no root of resentment springs up and causes trouble, and by it many be defiled.
HEBREWS 12:15 AMP

*A*hh, a fresh basket of autumn apples can be so satisfying. So colorful and crisp and fragrant. But if you're not careful, there could be some trouble brewing in the middle. One of the apples may be rotten—yeah, there's that whole off-gassing thing, as well as some mold brewing, not to mention a ravenous worm! Yes, your whole mini harvest may be threatened from one bad apple.

And so it goes with the influence of one resentful and rancorous person in our lives. A whole group can be corrupted with bitterness just like that basket of apples. Could it be that the rotten apple is you? Not possible, you say?

But do we ever get embittered and spew foul words and actions that have the potential to ruin the beauty of what God has done in our lives and in the lives of those around us?

May we ever flee from such behavior and instead exude the sweet fragrance of Christ's love and mercy!

———◆———

Father, show me when I become bitter, that I might not lead any of Your children astray. In Jesus' name I pray, amen. —A.H.

Fooled

*So Moses and Aaron went to Pharaoh and did just as the L*ORD *commanded. Aaron threw his staff down in front of Pharaoh and his officials, and it became a snake. Pharaoh then summoned wise men and sorcerers, and the Egyptian magicians also did the same things by their secret arts: Each one threw down his staff and it became a snake. But Aaron's staff swallowed up their staffs.*

EXODUS 7:10–12 NIV

*D*on't be fooled. There is still sorcery in the world, and it has power, as it did in the days of Pharaoh. Yes, it may arrive with some enticing new names, and its power is limited, but it still comes from the hand of the enemy and it's still just as deadly spiritually.

Christians are being fooled not only by false prophets but by various healing arts that are not biblically based. When in doubt about a particular treatment or practice that has roots in ancient philosophies, pray to the Holy Spirit for discernment and test all things through the Word of God. That way, we are not taken in by the temptations of the enemy who masquerades as an angel of light and will promise us anything to gain a foothold in our lives.

This is yet another good reason to walk closely with our Lord, to stay focused on His Word, and to fellowship with other Christians.

———◆———

Lord, this world is a dangerous place spiritually.
Please help me to cling to Your wisdom in all I do. Amen. —A.H.

A Woman of Grace

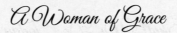

The one who has knowledge uses words with restraint,
and whoever has understanding is even-tempered.
PROVERBS 17:27 NIV

*S*ome people can't seem to help themselves when it comes to the gift of gab. They arrive on the scene with this never-ending supply of yak. When you're in line at the store. At parties. On social media. During your lunch hour at work. Next to you in the church pew. Everywhere. People have the ability to spew forth gossip, judgments, pontifications, speculations, and a wide range of blather—enough jibber-jabber to make your leg twitch and your eyes scan for the nearest exit door!

By the end of the day, we can be exhausted from too much of a bad thing—that is, worthless hot air that isn't taking anyone anywhere, certainly not lifted upward in a pretty balloon!

We learn in Proverbs 17 that people who have knowledge use restraint when they speak. They are not overflowing with a constant flow of chatter. People would rather gather around wise folk who are good listeners and who are even tempered. They will be a blessing to all those around them. Wouldn't all women, all people, long to be more like that?

———◆———

Dear Lord, I want to know when to speak up and when to remain
quiet. Help me to grow into a woman of grace. Amen. —A.H.

What Shall We Do Today, Father?

*He has made everything beautiful and appropriate in its time. He has also
planted eternity [a sense of divine purpose] in the human heart [a mysterious
longing which nothing under the sun can satisfy, except God]—yet man
cannot find out (comprehend, grasp) what God has done
(His overall plan) from the beginning to the end.*

ECCLESIASTES 3:11 AMP

Do you love creating things of beauty? Maybe an oil painting of a meadow that seems so real that the bumblebee looks like it will whirl right out of the picture? Or a spectacular work of architecture that becomes a beacon of beauty, lighting up the streets of the city? Or perhaps a melody so achingly beautiful that it warms one's heart every time it is heard.

We love to create things, not just art, but great works that use our gifts and talents. Works that not only connect us to our Creator but that fulfill our divine purpose on this earth. The Lord has indeed planted eternity in the human heart—that mysterious longing, which nothing under the sun can satisfy, except God. Aah yes, this is happiness.

---

*Lord, I want to do life with You always at my side. What wonderful
thing can we make together today? I'm excited
about all the possibilities! Amen. —A.H.*

Her Ways Are Pleasant Ways

Her ways are pleasant ways, and all her paths are peace. She is a tree of life
to those who take hold of her; those who hold her fast will be blessed.

PROVERBS 3:17–18 NIV

*J*f you asked a roomful of people, "Hey, who wants to come forward to receive a pleasant life, a pathway to peace, and the promise of blessings?" you might get trampled as people ran forward to receive these amazing gifts.

But how many times have we instead chosen sinful folly, which brought us the opposite of a pleasant life? Too many times to even count? The description of wisdom in Proverbs is winsome and irresistible. Yes, who can refuse? Since it pleases God for us to ask for wisdom as King Solomon did, may we never fail to ask the Lord for this precious treasure of the soul.

Yes, may we learn from our many errors and repent from our sins. May we pray to the Lord and ask Him that we rest under this beautiful tree of life called wisdom!

———◆———

Lord, I am at my wit's end. Life has become too complicated,
dangerous, and confusing. Please give me Your divine wisdom
in all my comings and goings. I need You now!
In Jesus' name I pray, amen. —A.H.

A Portrait of Grace

The son said to him, "Father, I have sinned against heaven and against you.
I am no longer worthy to be called your son." But the father said to his servants,
"Quick! Bring the best robe and put it on him. Put a ring on his finger and
sandals on his feet. Bring the fattened calf and kill it. Let's have a feast
and celebrate. For this son of mine was dead and is alive again;
he was lost and is found." So they began to celebrate.

LUKE 15:21–24 NIV

The parable of the Prodigal Son is a very popular Bible story. Why? Because it is such a beautiful portrait of grace. Our spirits sing to know that God loves us just like the earthly father loves his wayward son in this story.

The truth is we are all the prodigal son, in one way or another. All of us willfully want to go our own way at times. Humans can be so headstrong! But then we discover—the hard way—that we know nothing about how to care for ourselves, least of all spiritually. We are too busy chasing shifting shadows of pleasures while we miss what is true light and truth and beauty right before us.

The good news is—we can not only appreciate and admire God's portrait of grace, but through Christ, we can live it!

Thank You, Lord, for Your life-changing
mercy and grace! Amen. —A.H.

Running on Fumes

The Lord our God is merciful and forgiving,
even though we have rebelled against him.

DANIEL 9:9 NIV

*H*ave you ever felt like you're running on fumes? That you have given and loved and supported and been a servant to the point of exhaustion? Then—in the midst of that weariness—someone treats you shabbily?

It will happen. And when it does, tell God about it. He is the Master listener. The Master counselor. In fact, He is the master of all!

God knows just what we need in that moment, but it may not be what we expect. Perhaps the Lord wants us to take humility to a new level. He may teach us how to forgive what is hard to forgive. He may show us how to love the unlovable. To offer grace when all we really want to do is groan and scream and deliver a sharp comeback.

Ask and the Lord will show you what to do. Later you might think, *Okay, I have humbled myself. I have forgiven. I have offered grace. But I'm still running on fumes.* Tell God that too. He is merciful, and He'll send just the right person across your path to encourage you.

———————◆———————

Lord, I love You even when I don't understand this life. I want to do
life Your way, even when it's painful sometimes. Amen. —A.H.

Where Is the Real Power?

I can do all things [which He has called me to do] through Him who strengthens and empowers me [to fulfill His purpose—I am self-sufficient in Christ's sufficiency; I am ready for anything and equal to anything through Him who infuses me with inner strength and confident peace.]
PHILIPPIANS 4:13 AMP

Imagine a warm, brilliant radiance filling the room. Now imagine reaching over and unplugging the big lamp that supplied that light. Suddenly you are plunged into darkness so deep, you cannot even see your hand in front of you. You stumble through the room, desperately trying to be self-sufficient, pridefully attempting to go it alone without the light.

That is what happens when we embrace the enemy's lies—the notion of "inner power" without the Lord's presence in our lives. The book of Philippians reminds us that we can indeed do all things with Christ working through us. But it is Christ alone who empowers us. He is the One who infuses us with a supernatural strength and a confident peace so that we are ready for anything.

May we always plug ourselves into the true Source of all things—Jesus Christ.

Lord, may I never look to anything or anyone else for my strength, but You alone. In Jesus' holy name I pray, amen. —A.H.

Sooo Not a Good Look

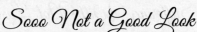

Let your gentle spirit [your graciousness, unselfishness, mercy, tolerance, and patience] be known to all people. The Lord is near.

PHILIPPIANS 4:5 AMP

Okay, so your best friend has a new look that makes you cringe. Her skin tight pants are so constricting, you wonder how she takes a deep breath. And they're the color of chartreuse! Her pants are so loud, in fact, that they are screaming at you. You're desperate to be a true friend and say, "Honey, that is sooo not a good look on you. Let me give you a helping hand."

But much worse than a bad new look is when she shows up with a bad new 'tude. Has your friend ever shown up in such a loud and foul mood that it makes you cringe for her? She bulldozes into the room, being harsh and impatient, and just about anything but gentle. You want to be a true friend and say, "Honey, that is sooo not a good look on you. Let me give you a helping hand."

But could it ever be that the friend in need of a helping hand—is me or you?

Oh Lord, I see it clearly now. Sometimes I am the monster who shows up with an attitude that is anything but gracious. Please forgive me. I want to be more like You and reflect Your goodness and mercy! Amen. —A.H.

Suffering Will Not Last

*He was despised and rejected by men, a Man of sorrows and pain and
acquainted with grief; and like One from whom men hide their faces.
He was despised, and we did not appreciate His worth or esteem Him.*

ISAIAH 53:3 AMP

*W*hen life seems to hit you with its worst blow and its darkest hour,
sometimes friends and family don't know what to say or do. They
mean well when they come to comfort you, but when they say, "I know how
you feel," the words ring hollow at best.

What can really be said in these times of despair? What can bring solace
when all of life falls apart? When the last light of hope seems to get snuffed out?

Know that Jesus was called a Man of sorrows. He knew temptation,
abandonment, loss, grief, humiliation, and the worst pain and suffering this
life can give. He felt it all—for you, for me. Take comfort in knowing that
this Man of sorrows is by your side, and that He really does know how you
feel. Know too that suffering will not last forever, but we will one day be
released from these frail bodies and our darkest hours will be no more. We
will enter into the glorious light of heaven!

---

*Jesus, I love You. Thank You for being ever near me in my time
of trouble, for being my Lord and Savior, and for giving
me the hope of heaven. Amen. —A.H.*

Illuminate My Life

*Your statutes are wonderful; therefore I obey them. The unfolding of your words
gives light; it gives understanding to the simple. I open my mouth
and pant, longing for your commands.*

PSALM 119:129–131 NIV

On that delight-filled day when you go to the eye doctor for a new pair of designer glasses, you usually hear a lot of, "So, which line is clearer? One or two?" That little Q&A goes back and forth, until that merry moment when you are handed a prescription for new glasses. Hopefully you will not only look cool, but you will see life more clearly.

When your eyesight goes from blurry to clear, wow, how enlightening! You see cobwebs in your house that you'd never seen before, as well as dirty bits of things here and there. But you also suddenly see what is beautiful too—the leaves on the trees and the smiles on faces. And perhaps now you won't stumble around so much.

Could this analogy be a bit like our spiritual lives and the Word of God? Do we read it daily for spiritual clarity so that we won't stumble on our journey or fall into a pothole of sin? Or so that we won't miss the beautiful gifts God has given us? May we all see life more clearly with the illumination of God's living Word!

—◆—

Lord, please light my path and my life with Your truths! Amen. —A.H.

Real Prayers for Real People

*The righteous cry out, and the L*ORD* hears them; he delivers them from all their troubles. The L*ORD* is close to the brokenhearted and saves those who are crushed in spirit.*

PSALM 34:17–18 NIV

When it's just you and God, are your prayers as pretty and graceful sounding as they are around the dinner table or when you're asked to pray at church? Perhaps they are prayers that go to the bone of your travails. You don't hold back. Your prayers become raw and real, and maybe even come with a trembling heartbeat and a bucket of tears. Is that you sometimes?

Well, you're not alone.

God tells us in His Word that when the righteous cry out He hears them. He is close to those who are brokenhearted and crushed in spirit. Those cries of the heart don't drift out into the wind never to be heard. God is our mighty deliverer. Trust Him and praise His mighty name!

———◆———

Thank You, Lord, for allowing me to be me, for letting me cry out to You when I'm in pain, when I'm discouraged, and when I am frightened of this world. I want to learn to trust You every hour of every day. Amen. —A.H.

His Loving Arms of Grace

"If a man has a hundred sheep, and one wanders away and is lost, what will he do?
Won't he leave the ninety-nine others and go out into the hills to search for
the lost one? And if he finds it, he will rejoice over it more than over the
ninety-nine others safe at home! Just so, it is not my Father's
will that even one of these little ones should perish."

MATTHEW 18:12–14 TLB

On a distant hill there is a lost lamb, and in its weariness, it is almost ready to tumble off a rocky cliff. The poor thing is hungry and frightened and doesn't know where to turn. It starts to bleat loudly. The shepherd hears the cry and leaves the herd to go in search of his beloved sheep. When he finds the lamb, he picks it up and carries it in the curve of his arm, very near his heart. The shepherd rejoices over finding his beloved sheep, as he carries it safely back home.

Christ—the Good Shepherd—will do the same for us. When we have drifted away and we are about to tumble off into the abyss of sin and despair, He still loves us. If we cry out to Him, the Lord will rescue us, offer us His loving arms of grace, and carry us safely home.

Lord Jesus, thank You for coming to get me when
I'm weary and I've lost my way. Amen. —A.H.

A Thousand Suns from Now

He has shown you, O mortal, what is good. And what does the Lord require of you? To act justly and to love mercy and to walk humbly with your God.
MICAH 6:8 NIV

*H*ave you ever wondered what you might be like a thousand suns from now? What will you look like, act like? How will other people see you? How will your relationships be with your loved ones? With your God? Will you walk so closely with the Lord that you can hear His voice? Will you cling to His holy precepts because you've learned that they will bring joy and peace? Will you act justly, love mercy, and walk humbly with your God?

Or will you still fly through your days with a frantic heart, still striving on your own? When the world is whirling out of control, will you choose fear or faith? Will you have learned how to have a servant's heart and a winsome and companionate spirit? Will you have fought the good fight?

Yes, in those thousands of days and nights from now, will you have grown into a woman of love and grace? May the answer be a resounding yes!

———◆———

Oh Lord, I want to hear Your voice and follow You. Please make me into the woman You created me to be! In Jesus' holy name I pray, amen. —A.H.

In Closing. . .

The amazing grace of the Master, Jesus Christ,
the extravagant love of God, the intimate friendship
of the Holy Spirit, be with all of you.

2 CORINTHIANS 13:14 MSG

Anita Higman, an award-winning author from Texas, enjoys traveling to exotic places, Spanish TV dramas, antiquing, fairy-tale everything, gardening (even though she has no idea what she's doing), all things Jane Austen, making brunch for her friends, and writing with Marian Leslie for the past few years! Please feel free to contact Anita Higman through her website at www.anitahigman.com. She would love to hear from you!

Marian Leslie is a writer and freelance editor. Though Marian has lived in southwestern Ohio for much of her life, she has ventured far and wide through the pages of many good books.

How God Grows a Woman of Faith

How God Grows a Woman of Faith is a devotional designed to enhance your spiritual journey. Featuring two hundred–plus devotional readings complemented by scripture selections and prayers, this lovely collection offers a powerful blend of inspiration, encouragement, and motivation for every area of your spiritual life.

Hardback / 978-1-68322-602-4 / $12.99

How God Grows a Girl of Grace

Use with Your Copy for Mommy and Me Study Time!
Featuring 180 devotional readings complemented by easy-to-understand scripture selections and prayers, this delightful collection offers a powerful blend of inspiration, encouragement, and godly guidance for girls ages 8 to 12. Girls will be motivated to spend one-on-one time with God as they read about topics that are important to them.

Paperback / 978-1-68322-322-1 / $4.99

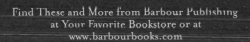